"Every generation of chu___ ___ ___ ___ ___ ___ ___ ___ ___ ple of God must exercis_ ___ ___ ___ ___ ___ ___ ___ ___ pass on the truth to the ___. ___ ___ ___ ___ ___ ___ seen countless men and women capitulate God's truth in exchange for cultural relevancy. Spineless is the manifesto we so desperately need. Thoroughly biblical, David Steele has served the church well by setting courage and conviction as the necessary virtues that will ensure that believers never surrender the high ground of God's truth in Christ."

DR. DUSTIN BENGE

Provost and Professor of Church History, Union School of Theology, Bridgend, Wales

"This is a timely call from Pastor Steele to avoid, in a time of great opposition to the Christian faith, the sin Christians fall into of passivity and cowardice. It is a helpful reminder of the importance of staying rooted in Scripture and being helped by the example of heroes of the faith, like the OT prophets, the apostles, the Reformers, the Huguenots, and the Puritans. Also being instructed by theologians like Luther, Calvin, Bavinck, Martyn Lloyd-Jones, J.I. Packer, C. S. Lewis, Francis Schaeffer and Al Mohler in his book, The Gathering Storm. Specifically, strong Christians must settle the matter of worldviews, and be aware of the stark contrast between biblical Christianity and false religious and philosophical systems of our day, knowing that only the Christian worldview is sufficient."

DR. PETER JONES

Director, TruthXchange; author of The Other Worldview, Escondido, CA

"Spineless is a call for courageous and convictional Christianity in the midst of an evangelicalism that is often more prone to capitulation than to fearless proclamation. Author David Steele, identifies the problems afflicting both the church and the world but he is not content to simply "curse the darkness;" he shines the light back to the path of courageous Christianity. The need is great. The stakes are high. The time is now to stand up for truth and to stand confidently on God's inerrant Word. Steele skillfully utilizes history, theology, and worldview scholarship as he illustrates the biblical call to courage. This book is biblical, timely, and needed. You will learn, grow, and be challenged to a life of courageous faithfulness. I recommend this excellently written work."

DR. RAY RHODES. JR.

Author of *Yours, Till Heaven: The Untold Love Story of Charles and Susie Spurgeon* and *Susie: The Life and Legacy of Susannah Spurgeon*

"My comrade in ministry has hit another homerun with this book. One of the most detrimental quotes attributed to Francis of Assisi so many Christians have latched onto is the saying, "Preach the gospel at all times and when necessary, use words." Dr. Steele balances this ancient pragmatism with the facts that those who have most, and will most transform society are those who know the Word, are convinced and convicted of its authority and truth, and apply it daily in their thoughts, hearts, actions and proclamation of the gospel. Never more than today do we need men and women of conviction that know their Bibles and proclaim and live its message boldly with grace and truth. Thanks again, Dr. Steele for such a motivational manifesto to be theologically and theocentrically courageous in our time by speaking and proclaiming the gospel clearly and loudly."

DR. DAVID P. CRAIG

Lead Pastor, Valley Baptist Church, San Rafael, CA

"In his latest book, Spineless: Restoring Courage and Conviction to the People of God, David Steele takes readers by the hand and guides them as only a pastor-theologian par excellence can into the rich soil of biblical-theological convictions that will help shape their lives. In our day, we need Christians who are unafraid of the truth and unashamed to stand upon God's Word. David, in this work not only gives the correct diagnosis, but the remedy to the ills of why many Christians lack a backbone by steadying our gaze upon the biblical text and the person and work of Jesus Christ. By doing so, he helps his readers discover from the Bible and Church History how men and women of God have stood upon the truth of God's Word with courage and conviction. Wherever you are at in your walk with the Lord and whatever station you have in the church reading, Spineless will help you grow and be shaped by the Word of God, for a life lived under the gaze of God, for the glory of God."

DAVE JENKINS

Executive Director, Servants of Grace Ministries, Executive Editor, Theology for Life Magazine, Host, Equipping You in Grace, Teacher, Servants of Grace and Warrior of Grace Podcasts

"Drawing from the rich legacy of bold and courageous men of church history, and chock-full of sound biblical teaching, Spineless is a must read for all Christians who desire to boldly live with courage and conviction in an age of timidity and rampant compromise."

JEREMY PICKENS

Senior Pastor, Good Shepherd Church, Ferndale, WA

"I not only highly recommend this book to you, but just as importantly, its author. Dr. David Steele doesn't just write words well, he lives them out. His character is worthy of emulating and his writings should be read and reflected on. We need more men like Pastor Steele, men of Gospel grit, who confront our age's spinelessness with courage and boldness."

BRYAN PICHURA

Senior Pastor, Mount Olivet Church, Huron, SD

"The negative effects of pride and domineering church leadership have been well documented, but not enough has been said and written about the perils of cowardice and passivity. Drawing from Scripture, church history, and personal life experience, Dr. David Steele pens a well-researched book for Christians to get serious about being men and women of courage. The amount of relevant church history references in this book is stunning. It's the kind of book that will be particularly suitable for young Christians."

DAVID QAOUD

Associate Pastor, Blogger, Bethesda Evangelical Church, St. Louis, MO, gospelrelevance.com

SPINELESS

RESTORING COURAGE AND CONVICTION TO THE PEOPLE OF GOD

DAVID S. STEELE

TO J.C. RYLE,

A lion of God and stalwart of the faith who lived with all his might, faithfully proclaiming the truth no matter the cost and fearless in the midst of the flames. For leading courageously and living according to his convictions. For faithfully wielding the sword of truth in the pulpit and always willing to stand with courage in the pyre.

CONTENTS

⋙ INTRODUCTION ⋘

...

We live in an age of unprecedented compromise. Courage has been eclipsed by cowardice. Conviction has been highjacked by capitulation. The bishop of Liverpool, J.C. Ryle (1816-1900) lamented the lack of courage and conviction that characterized so many Christians in the United Kingdom. He bemoaned the cowardice that dominated the theological landscape, especially among young people:

> *It produces what I must venture to call a 'jellyfish' Christianity in the land: that is, a Christianity without bone, or muscle, or power. A jellyfish is a pretty and graceful object when it floats in the sea, contracting and expanding like a little, delicate, transparent umbrella. Yet the same jellyfish, when cast on the shore, is a mere helpless lump, without capacity for movement, self-defense, or self-preservation. Alas! It is a vivid type of much of the religion of the day, of which the leading principle is, 'No dogma, no distinct tenets, no positive doctrine.'*[1]

---

[1] J.C. Ryle, *Principles for Churchmen* (London: William Hunt, 1884), 97-98. Cited in J.I. Packer, *Faithfulness and Holiness* (Wheaton: Crossway Books, 2002), 72.

FAREWELL TO THE JELLYFISH

Tragically, not much has changed. The church in the twenty-first century can accurately be described as *spineless*. Simply put, we have lost our courage. We are weak-kneed and fearful. We bear a strange resemblance to the Cowardly Lion in *The Wizard of Oz*. When confronted by Dorothy for his fearful disposition, the Lion freely admits, "You're right, I am a coward. I haven't any courage at all. I even scare myself!" Such is the state of the contemporary church. R. Albert Mohler remarks, "Where the church fails to declare the truth, it forfeits its status as a true church. When churches capitulate and compromise the truth, they betray their status as part of God's people."[2] Sadly, many of our churches find themselves in the compromised position that Mohler describes. We have lost our nerve. We lack a backbone. We are spineless.

The contemporary church is in great need of courage and conviction. Very few Christ-followers possess the fiery faith of the Puritans. We desperately lack the bold resolve of the Reformers. We are unwilling to draw theological "lines in the sand." We are not prepared to stand for truth with men like Polycarp, Cranmer, Knox, or Tyndale. Instead, we are geared to pleasing men, appealing to the lowest common denominator, and making people "happy," no matter the cost. We are milktoast Christians; theological lightweights. We are spineless.

Philip Graham Ryken, in addressing the apostasy of Israel, poses a sobering question: "What verdict would God render about the contemporary church? The dominant sin of Jerusalem—forgetting God—has become a predominant sin in the American church."[3]

Has a nation changed its gods? But my people have changed their glory for that which does not profit. Be appalled, O heavens, at this; be shocked, be utterly desolate, declares the LORD, for my people have committed two evils: they have

[2] R. Albert Mohler, *The Apostles' Creed: Discovering Authentic Christianity in an Age of Counterfeits* (Nashville: Nelson Books, 2019), 153.
[3] Philip Graham Ryken, *Courage to Stand: Jeremiah's Message for Post-Christian Times* (Philipsburg: Presbyterian & Reformed, 1998), 25.

forsaken me, the fountain of living waters, and hewed out cisterns for themselves, broken cisterns that can hold no water (Jer. 2:11-13).

And now what do you gain by going to Egypt to drink the waters of the Nile? Or what do you gain by going to Assyria to drink the waters of the Euphrates? Your evil will chastise you, and your apostasy will reprove you. Know and see that it is evil and bitter for you to forsake the LORD your God; the fear of me is not in you, declares the LORD GOD of hosts (Jer. 2:18-19).

In the opening verses of Isaiah 1, God admonishes Judah for her sin: "Ah, sinful nation, a people laden with iniquity, offspring of evildoers, children who deal corruptly! They have forsaken the LORD, they have despised the Holy One of Israel, they are utterly estranged" (Isa. 1:4).

Throughout the first five chapters of Isaiah, the southern kingdom of Judah is admonished for her sin:

They were rebellious

Hear, O heavens, and give ear, O earth; for the LORD has spoken: 'Children have I reared and brought up, but they have rebelled against me' (Isa. 1:2).

Why will you still be struck down? Why will you continue to rebel? The whole head is sick, and the whole heart is faint (Isa. 1:5).

Their sin had rendered them filthy

Wash yourselves; make yourselves clean; remove the evil of your deeds from before my eyes; cease to do evil (Isa. 1:16).

They were unfaithful and failed to render justice to the oppressed

How the faithful city has become a whore, she who was full of justice! Righteousness lodged in her, but now murderers. Your silver has become dross, your best wine mixed with water. Your princes are rebels and companions of thieves. Everyone loves a bribe and runs after gifts. They do not bring justice to the fatherless, and the widow's cause does not come to them (Isa.1:21–23).

They were idolaters

Their land is filled with idols; they bow down to the work of their hands, to what their own fingers have made (Isa. 2:8).

They were filled with arrogance

The haughty looks of man shall be brought low, and the lofty pride of men shall be humbled, and the LORD alone will be exalted in that day (Isa. 2:11).

They disrespected authority figures

And the people will oppress one another, every one his fellow and every one his neighbor; the youth will be insolent to the elder, and the despised to the honorable (Isa. 3:5).

They were blasphemers

For Jerusalem has stumbled, and Judah has fallen, because their speech and their deeds are against the LORD, defying his glorious presence (Isa. 3:8).

Like God's people in the Old Testament, the twenty-first-century church has lost its bearings and has forsaken God. We have caved in and capitulated to contemporary culture. Indeed, we have "married the spirit of the age" and as Dean Inge suggests, "we have become the widower."[4] The lampstand has been concealed. Our light has been snuffed out. We have lost our influence. We are spineless.

RECASTING RYLE'S LAMENT

The cowardice in the church was originally challenged by J.C. Ryle in nineteenth-century England. The cultural context was different, to be sure. Tragically, the cowardice in the contemporary church only continues to escalate. Our ecclesiastical malady

---

[4] See Os Guinness, *The Last Christian on Earth: Uncover the Enemy's Plot to Undermine the Church* (Grand Rapids: Baker Books), 200.

would have troubled Ryle to no end. The propensity to tone down doctrinal propositions was and is not only a problem among people in the pew; it poses a challenge to church leaders as well. The former Bishop of Liverpool writes candidly and persuasively:

We have hundreds of 'jellyfish' clergymen, who seem not to have a single bone in their body of divinity. They have no definite opinions; they belong to no school or party; they are so afraid of 'extreme views' that they have no views at all. We have thousands of 'jellyfish' sermons preached every year, sermons without an edge, or a point, or a corner, smooth as billiard balls, awakening no sinner, and edifying no saint. We have Legions of 'jellyfish' young men annually turned out from our Universities, armed with a few scraps of second-hand philosophy, who think it a mark of cleverness and intellect to have no decided opinions about anything in religion, and to be utterly unable to make up their minds as to what is Christian truth.[5]

This is precisely the kind of mentality that has crept into the present-day church. This mindset of mediocrity is weakening the church and draining the spiritual fervor and zeal of God's people. This "spineless" Christianity has become the new norm, which values tolerance over truth and pragmatism over preaching. It celebrates diversity in the name of unity and subtly destroys the faithful adherence to the truth of the gospel. Ryle concludes his lament by focusing his attention on the church at large:

Worst of all, we have myriads of 'jellyfish' worshippers —respectable church-going people, who have no distinct views about any point in theology. They cannot discern things that differ, any more than color-blind people can distinguish colors. They think everybody is right and nobody wrong, everything is true and nothing is false, all sermons are good and none are bad, every clergyman is sound and no clergyman is unsound. They are 'tossed to and fro, like children, by every wind of doctrine,' often carried

[5] J.C. Ryle, *Principles for Churchmen*, 97-98. Cited in J.I. Packer, *Faithfulness and Holiness*, 72-73.

away by any new excitement and sensational movement; ever ready for new things, because they have no firm grasp on the old; and utterly unable to 'render a reason of the hope that is in them.' [6]

Ryle's complaint with the church is as relevant now as it was in the nineteenth-century. Instead of strong convictions, many professing Christ-followers are spineless. We see compromise at every level: doctrinal compromise, financial compromise, ethical compromise, and sexual compromise. It appears that nothing is out of bounds. Everything is accepted. Every lifestyle is tolerated. The postmodern milieu simply has no room for the transcendent, unchanging standards of God's word. "Apparently the M. Div does not come with a backbone," says Douglas Wilson in a recent podcast. We bear a strange resemblance to ancient Israel: "In those days there was no king in Israel. Everyone did what was right in his own eyes" (Judg. 21:25).

AN URGENT CALL

A.W. Tozer writes, "A scared world needs a fearless church."[7] Now is the time, then, for Christ-followers to shore up their biblical convictions and wage the good warfare (1 Tim. 1:18). It is time for a reformation of biblical courage and conviction. In 2017, churches around the world celebrated the five-hundredth anniversary of the Protestant Reformation and commemorated the courage of Martin Luther. Because Luther held tenaciously to his biblical convictions, he was both a hated man and a hunted man.

After his now celebrated Ninety-five Theses were posted and went viral, Luther was on the run for most of the rest of his life. As he made his way to the Diet of Worms in 1521, he saw the imperial notices which were posted and condemned his views. One of his traveling companions asked if he wanted to

---

[6] Ibid, 73.

[7] A.W. Tozer, *This World: Playground or Battleground?* (Chicago: Moody Publishers, 1989), Kindle edition, loc 103-118.

continue on the journey. Luther's response was to remain steadfast but "did so with trembling."[8]

What gave Luther the strength and courage to act with such bold resolve? Here's what we find: Luther was a man of unshakeable *courage* and *conviction*. It was *courage* and *conviction* that led Luther to hammer the Ninety-five Theses to the Castle door at Wittenberg. It was *courage* and *conviction* that enabled him to stand before the Holy Roman Empire at the Imperial Diet of Worms. It was *courage* and *conviction* that drove Luther to translate the Greek New Testament into German at the Wartburg castle.[9]

From Wittenberg to Worms to Wartburg, we find a man who knew what he believed and was willing to act on those beliefs. Like Luther, it is time to *act* on our beliefs. It is time to say, "Farewell to the jellyfish!"

B.B. Warfield (1851-1921) understood the importance of courage and conviction in the Christian life:

> *Convictions are the root on which the tree of vital Christianity grows. No convictions, no Christianity. Scanty convictions, hunger-bitten Christianity. Profound convictions, solid and substantial religion. Let no man fancy it can be otherwise. Ignorance is not the mother of religion, but of irreligion. The knowledge of God is eternal life, and to know God means that we know him aright.[10]*

Spineless: Restoring Courage and Conviction to the People of God addresses the insipid kind of "Christianity" that has slipped into the church. In part one, we'll *diagnose the decline of courage and conviction*. We shall not only trace its tragic demise; we shall underscore a hidden concern, namely, the fear factor. But diagnosing this troubling trend is only the beginning.

---

[8] Cited in Herman Selderhuis, *Martin Luther: A Spiritual Biography* (Wheaton: Crossway, 2017), 153.

[9] See David S. Steele, *Bold Reformer: Celebrating the Gospel-Centered Convictions of Martin Luther* (Houston: Lucid Books, 2016).

[10] http://irbsseminary.org/b-b-warfield-faith-life-sound-distinctions-importance-preaching/

In part two, we shall begin to put the pieces in place that will lead to the *recovery of courage and conviction*. Here we will learn some of the key ingredients that Christians must build into their lives in order to move forward with biblical courage and conviction.

Finally, in part three, we will present *the rally cry of courage and conviction*. We will take a careful look at the war that we're engaged in and present biblical strategies for restoring our spiritual muscle.

Several years ago, I sat next to my father at the Shepherds' Conference in Sun Valley, California. Dr. Steven Lawson was addressing a packed house in a message entitled "Bring the Book," an exposition of Nehemiah 8:1-6. It was a sermon that marked my soul and forever changed my life and ministry. In the course of that sermon, Lawson uttered these words that I later learned were originally attributed to Dr. John MacArthur: "Now is the time for the strongest men to preach the strongest message in the context of the strongest ministry." These pivotal words are inscribed in my preaching Bible to remind me that anything less than Spirit-inspired courage and conviction is unacceptable for a disciple of Jesus Christ. Anything less is tantamount to weak and compromised lives, churches, and ministries.

So farewell to the jellyfish. May the next generation of pastors and Christian leaders work together to restore gospel-centered courage and conviction. May we stand together with bold resolve and raise the banner in honor of our sovereign king. May the days of spineless Christian leaders perish and may biblical courage and conviction define a new generation of leaders in the church of Jesus Christ!

 PART 1

DIAGNOSING THE DECLINE OF COURAGE
AND CONVICTION

--- ... ---

"The only thing we have to fear is fear itself."

President Franklin D. Roosevelt

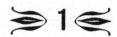

THE DEMISE OF COURAGE AND CONVICTION

"When Saul and all Israel heard these words from the Philistine, they lost their courage and were terrified."

1 Samuel 17:11, CSB

Whenen a band of American rebels gathered in Philadelphia to discuss waging war against the British Crown by signing the *Declaration of Independence*, they understood that failure would be met by a charge of treason and death by hanging. For this reason, the group remained divided for a season as they came to terms with their passion to pursue the dream of independence. Benjamin Franklin understood the risks that lay ahead. Even so, he famously urged a spirit of courage and unanimity: "We must, indeed, all hang together—or most assuredly we will hang separately." Indeed, the American people stand on the shoulders of men who demonstrated uncanny courage in the face of adversity. The steely resolve of the founding fathers' breathe courage into our souls and instill deep conviction in our bones.

STANDING ON THE SHOULDERS OF THE COURAGEOUS

In church history, we stand on the shoulders of the great titans of the faith who lived what they believed and prioritized truth over the convenience of pragmatism. Some died of natural causes but faced constant persecution and even the threat of death—men like Luther, Calvin, and Spurgeon. Others actually gave their lives because of their convictions—men like Polycarp, William Tyndale, Jan Hus, and John Rogers.

These great stalwarts of the Christian faith teach us how to endure the trials of life and the flames of persecution. "Indeed, all who desire to live a godly life in Christ Jesus will be persecuted" (2 Tim. 3:12). The likes of William Cowper, John Calvin, and Charles Haddon Spurgeon endured physical pain most of their adult lives. For instance, Spurgeon battled kidney disease and horrible bouts of depression.

John Calvin endured more persecution during his ministry years than most people will see in a lifetime. When he returned to pastor a flock in Geneva, the French Huguenots (Protestant saints from Scotland and England) who sought refuge from "Bloody Mary," fled to Calvin's Geneva. One of those refugees who sat under Calvin's teaching was John Knox, who called Calvin's church in Geneva, "the most perfect school of Christ that ever was in the earth since the days of the Apostles." Many of the pastors and leaders who were trained by Calvin were sent out to plant churches in Europe. Since persecution was commonplace and martyrdom a real possibility for these godly people, his school became known as "Calvin's School of Death."

We stand on the shoulders of those brave Christians who *knew* what they believed and *lived* what they believed. These lionhearted men and women were willing to act on the strength of their beliefs, no matter the cost. These were people of courage and conviction. Boldness, fearlessness, and fortitude defined their lives. When they were opposed, they stood strong. When persecuted they persisted. They stood alone when everyone else fled. They maintained their Christian valor when others acquiesced to the dictates of the world. These people stood with bold resolve and maintained the strength of their convictions, even in the midst of persecution and adversity.

THE EROSION OF COURAGE AND CONVICTION

But courage and conviction are certainly not the majority report. Cowardly people cave in at the first sight of difficulty and compromise when the future is uncertain. Convictions are jettisoned at the first sight of controversy. They have not yet been instilled with the fiery courage and conviction of the Reformers and Puritans. Their spineless posture is unmistakable and commonplace, yet their weakness finds its origin as far back as the mind can conceive.

The demise of courage and conviction begins, no doubt, with the fall of our first parents: "And the LORD God commanded the man, saying, "You may surely eat of every tree of the garden, but of the tree of the knowledge of good and evil you shall not eat, for in the day that you eat of it you shall surely die"" (Gen. 2:16–17). Let us call this *truth claim # 1*. God's directive is clear and unequivocal. His command needs no clarification. There is not of hint of ambiguity here. Any deviation from his mandate results in death—both physical death *and* spiritual death.

Truth claim # 2 comes directly from the mouth of the serpent. Instead of uttering divinely inspired truth as God did in Genesis 2:16-17, the serpent's claim to truth is a clever blend of wickedness and deceptiveness. He brazenly challenges God and questions his authority. He says to Eve, "You will not surely die. For God knows that when you eat of it your eyes will be opened, and you will be like God, knowing good and evil" (Gen. 3:4-5). Scripture recounts the original compromise with God's truth: "So when the woman saw that the tree was good for food, and that it was a delight to the eyes, and that the tree was to be desired to make one wise, she took of its fruit and ate, and she also gave some to her husband who was with her, and he ate" (Gen. 3:6).

All of this raises an important question: Where was Adam when his wife faced the fiery challenges of the serpent? Since Eve succumbed to the serpent's temptation and offered the forbidden fruit to Adam, it would appear that he was within a stone's throw of her. That being the case, we are forced to ask a series of additional questions:

1. Why didn't Adam intervene when the serpent questioned the authority of God?

2. Why didn't Adam make a bold stand when the serpent challenged the veracity of God?

3. Why didn't Adam lovingly lead his wife on the path of truth, submission, and obedience?

4. Why didn't Adam obey God?

The answer to each of these questions is that Adam was spineless. Adam's sin plunged the human race onto a collision course with death. Because of Adam's sin, each of us live under the curse. The curse brings spiritual darkness (Isa. 9:1; Eph. 2:12). And the curse brings spiritual death. "Therefore, just as sin came into the world through one man, and death through sin, and so death spread to all men because all sinned" (Rom. 5:12). As we shall discover, the curse of Adam's sin has deep spiritual implications that influence how we live, including our relationships and how we interact in our churches and in our communities.

A COLLISION COURSE WITH COWARDICE

One of the tragic trajectories of Adam's sin, especially among men, is the sin of passivity. The passage of time has failed to erase the effects of this deadly virus. On the contrary, there has been a steady slide of masculine passivity since the original sin in the Garden of Eden. Passivity, then, is tantamount to spinelessness. Men are increasingly passive and cowardly. Large numbers of Christian men are mimicking their father, Adam. They are failing to pick up the mantel of leadership that God has entrusted to them. The cost of their passivity is paid by wives, who are left to assume a leadership role that God never intended. And sinful male passivity leaves children on the desperate search for male role models and examples of godly living.

Dennis Rainey confronts the growing epidemic of passivity among men: "Male passivity is a disease that robs a man of his purpose while it destroys marriages, ruins families, and spoils legacies. A passive man doesn't engage, he retreats. He neglects personal responsibility. At its core, passivity is cowardice."[11] Passive men abdicate their responsibilities. Passive men blame anyone except themselves—parents, church, government, school, and friends. They resist accountability and shun anyone who address sin. Passive men oppose anyone who has the audacity to raise a high and holy standard. The bottom line: passive men are spineless.

EXAMPLES OF COWARDS IN SCRIPTURE

It should come as no surprise that Adam's son, Cain followed in his father's footsteps and proved himself to be a coward (Gen. 4). Motivated by jealousy, he murdered his brother, Abel in cold blood. When the LORD asked Cain about the whereabouts of Abel, his response was smug and dismissive: "I do not know; am I my brother's keeper?" Cain takes a page out of his father's playbook. He becomes an expert in hiding his sin and hurling his sin. This man plays the role of a coward. This man shuns accountability. This man refuses to live in the light or accept responsibility for his sin (Eph. 5:11-14).

God's response to Cain's sin is decisive: "And the LORD said, "What have you done? The voice of your brother's blood is crying to me from the ground. And now you are cursed from the ground, which has opened its mouth to receive your brother's blood from your hand. When you work the ground, it shall no longer yield to you its strength. You shall be a fugitive and a wanderer on the earth"" (Gen. 4:10–12). Cain responds to God with typical cowardice: "Cain said to the LORD, "My punishment is greater than I can bear" (Gen. 4:13). After God reaffirmed his commitment to justice, Cain "went away from the presence of the LORD and settled in the land of Nod, east of Eden" (Gen. 4:16).

---

[11] Dennis Rainey, *Stepping Up: A Call to Courageous Manhood* (Little Rock: Family Life Publishing, 2011), 44.

Another example of cowardice is Paul's ministry associate, Demas. He was loyal to the apostle Paul for a season, but in the end he proved to be unfaithful. J.C. Ryle underscores the sin of this spineless man:

> *For want of 'counting the cost,' Demas forsook the gospel, forsook Christ, forsook heaven. For a long time he journeyed with the great Apostle of the Gentiles, and was actually a 'fellow-laborer.' But when he found he could not have the friendship with this world as well as the friendship of God, he gave up his Christianity and clave to the world. 'Demas hath forsaken me,' says St. Paul, 'having loved this present world' (2 Tim. 4:10). He had not counted the cost.*[12]

Finally, consider the example of Achan. The Bible describes this man as a crook, someone who pillaged the spoils, which prompted God to be angry with Israel (Josh. 7:1). God reveals Achan's sin to Joshua and raises the stakes of accountability: "The LORD said to Joshua, 'Get up! Why have you fallen on your face? Israel has sinned; they have transgressed my covenant that I commanded them; they have taken some of the devoted things; they have stolen and lied and put them among their own belongings" (Josh 7:10-11). As the story continues, the gravity of Achan's sin is spelled out: "And he who is taken with the devoted things shall be burned with fire, he and all that he has, because he has transgressed the covenant of the LORD, and because he has done an outrageous thing in Israel" (Josh. 7:15).

When Joshua realizes the weightiness of Achan's sin, he confronts him, which led to a half-hearted confession:

> *Then Joshua said to Achan, 'My son, give glory to the LORD God of Israel and give praise to him. And tell me now what you have done; do not hide it from me.' And Achan answered Joshua, 'Truly I have sinned against the LORD God of Israel, and this is what I did: when I saw among the spoil a beautiful cloak from Shinar, and 200 shekels of silver,*

---

[12] J.C. Ryle, *Holiness: Its Nature, Hindrances, Difficulties, and Roots* (Edinburgh: The Banner of Truth Trust, 2014), 100.

*and a bar of gold weighing 50 shekels, then I coveted them
and took them. And see, they are hidden in the earth inside
my tent, with the silver underneath.' So Joshua sent messen-
gers, and they ran to the tent; and behold, it was hidden in
his tent with the silver underneath. And they took them out
of the tent and brought them to Joshua and to all the people
of Israel. And they laid them down before the LORD. And
Joshua and all Israel with him took Achan the son of Zerah,
and the silver and the cloak and the bar of gold, and his sons
and daughters and his oxen and donkeys and sheep and his
tent and all that he had. And they brought them up to the
Valley of Achor (Josh. 7:19–24).*

The story concludes on a bitter note as Achan is stoned by
the people: "And Joshua said, "Why did you bring trouble on us?
The LORD brings trouble on you today." And all Israel stoned
him with stones. They burned them with fire and stoned them
with stones. And they raised over him a great heap of stones that
remains to this day. Then the LORD turned from his burning
anger. Therefore, to this day the name of that place is called the
Valley of Achor" (Josh. 7:25–26).

THE DEMISE OF COURAGE AND CONVICTION

The tragic tales of Cain, Demas, and Achan are grim reminders
of the path and peril of cowardice. Tragically, the godless legacy
of these men are being perpetuated in our generation and do not
show any signs of slowing down. "Once beliefs have been min-
imized and convictions have been marginalized, energy leaves
the movement like air escaping a balloon."[13] Cowardly men and
women suck the spiritual vitality from unsuspecting people. Instead of leaving a legacy of Christ-saturated courage, these cowardly souls encourage a spirit of passivity and timidity, which is
annihilating the next generation of leaders.

While they may not intend to negatively influence the
next generation, their silence is hindering gospel effectiveness

---

[13] Albert Mohler, *The Conviction to Lead* (Minneapolis: Bethany House
Publishers, 2012), 55.

and world evangelization. "Silence or compromise," writes John MacArthur, "might mean a measure of comfort, acceptance, or even popularity. But it lacks integrity and smacks of cowardice and infidelity."[14] These spineless people not only fail to lead well; they promote a vacuous variety of "faith." Instead of living faithfully before God, they lead others astray. The parade of cowards continues the long march and contributes to the demise of courage and conviction.

---

[14] John MacArthur, *Remaining Faithful in Ministry: 9 Essential Convictions for Every Pastor* (Wheaton: Crossway, 2019), 65.

THE FEAR FACTOR

—— ••• ——

"Even though I walk through the valley of the shadow of death, I will fear no evil, for you are with me; your rod and your staff, they comfort me."

Psalm 23:4

I t was a warm, spring afternoon. I decided to steal away for a few hours to read and write at Starbucks. As I waited patiently for a cup of Seattle's finest, I noticed an elderly gentleman seated in the corner. This stately man wore a cap that proudly displayed his service in the United States military during World War II. I approached him, extended my hand, and introduced myself. He shook my hand firmly and looked me straight in the eye. "Sir, thank you for your service," I said with sincere appreciation and respect. He smiled warmly and replied, "You're very welcome, son. Thank you for your support."

My grandfather served in the Pacific theater during the dark days of World War II. He proudly described how the American military fought with courage to defend our freedom, dismantle Hitler's totalitarian regime, and destroy the Japanese dream of world domination. At the conclusion of the war, he lived through a very different kind of struggle known commonly as the Cold War. He lived in the days where nuclear proliferation was a daily possibility. He understood the threat of Marxism-Leninism, which has since been relegated into the "ash-heap" of history, as President Reagan promised.[15]

Our World War II veterans represent what is best about America—strength, honor, fortitude, patriotism, and faithfulness. They are marked by courage and conviction. But the generation who fought for our freedom is slowly slipping away. According to the US Department of Veterans Affairs statistics, we are losing 372 veterans per day and only 620,000 of the 16 million Americans who served in World War II were alive in 2016.[16] That number will decrease sharply over the next several years.

One day, America will awaken to a country where World War II veterans are only a distant dream. But losing these patriots is only part of the story. Along with the loss of these heroes comes a steady decline in courage and conviction. Let's face it —we live in a spineless culture. Instead of bold beliefs and brave resolve, our culture is dominated by cowardice and a lack of conviction.

But even worse, the loss of courage and conviction has also crept into the church. Fear of man has replaced a robust faith in God. And worldly beliefs have replaced confident convictions, which are rooted and grounded in God's Word. The *fear factor* has crippled our resolve and hindered our ability to minister in the postmodern world. Even as I write, a wave of left-wing political organizations are rising up and working hard to silence anyone who disagrees with their liberal and Marxist worldviews. Will anyone with courage and conviction stand up and face these evil aggressors or will their radical plot prevail?

FACING THE WOLVES

The first-century church faced a fearsome foe as she fought valiantly against false teachers. Our day is no different as the wolves at the gate continue to wreak havoc in the postmodern

---

[15] See Brett Baier, *Three Days in Moscow* (New York: HarperCollins Publishers, 2018), 124.

[16] https://www.nationalww2museum.org/about-us/frequently-asked-questions

milieu and infiltrate the contemporary church. The apostle Paul paints a portrait of godlessness in his letter to Timothy:

> But understand this, that in the last days there will come times of difficulty. For people will be lovers of self, lovers of money, proud, arrogant, abusive, disobedient to their parents, ungrateful, unholy, heartless, unappeasable, slanderous, without self-control, brutal, not loving good, treacherous, reckless, swollen with conceit, lovers of pleasure rather than lovers of God, having the appearance of godliness, but denying its power. Avoid such people. For among them are those who creep into households and capture weak women, burdened with sins and led astray by various passions, always learning and never able to arrive at a knowledge of the truth. Just as Jannes and Jambres opposed Moses, so these men also oppose the truth, men corrupted in mind and disqualified regarding the faith. But they will not get very far, for their folly will be plain to all, as was that of those two men (2 Tim. 3:1–9).

Paul warns the young pastor that wolves are prowling on the loose. These beasts pay no regard to the Word of God and work tirelessly to intimidate the people of God. They are marked by a spirit of autonomy. When Paul ministered to the Ephesian elders, he warned them to be on their guard against these predators: "I know that after my departure fierce wolves will come in among you, not sparing the flock; and from among your own selves will arise men speaking twisted things, to draw away the disciples after them" (Acts 20:29–30). Indeed, the wolves are prowling at the gate. These wolves, both then and now, are marked by some predictable characteristics. Recognizing these vicious beasts will be a crucial step in our journey away from spinelessness.

THE PROFILE OF A WOLF

Our generation understands the dangers of profiling. We have learned that categorizing a person or a people group on the basis of ethnicity, socio-economic status, or background is not only inappropriate, it is downright rude, and may even be tantamount to racism. But an exception must be granted when we consider wolves. Therefore, consider several characteristics of wolves that we are bound to encounter on our respective Christian journeys.

First, *wolves are ferocious*. Paul warns, "I know that after my departure fierce wolves will come in among you, not sparing the flock …" (Acts 20:29). The word translated *fierce* means "a troublemaker; a savage." Likewise, Jesus warns us: "Beware of false prophets, who come to you in sheep's clothing but inwardly are ravenous wolves" (Matt. 7:15). *Ravenous* comes from a Greek word that means "destructive, violent, or vicious." The same word may be applied to a stormy sea that rages out of control. So too, these ravenous wolves seek to strike the church and the followers of Jesus Christ with full force and they do so with reckless disregard. Is it any wonder that the saints are cowering in fear? Instead of standing strong in the face of adversity, many of Christ's blood-bought are left trembling. They are spineless.

These ferocious wolves are satanic ambassadors who do the bidding of the prince of darkness. They seek to hinder the work of the ministry (1 Thess. 2:18). They work with all their might to stir up pride in the people of God. For "pride goes before destruction, and a haughty spirit before a fall" (Prov. 16:18). Ultimately, their aim is to destroy the people of God. Jesus reminds us, "The thief comes only to steal and kill and destroy …" (John 10:10).

Second, *wolves are stealthy*. "I know that after my departure," writes Paul, "fierce wolves will come in among you, not sparing the flock" (Acts 20:29). A *stealthy* person operates in a way that prevents them from being seen or detected. In the early 90's, I remember strolling out of a guitar shop in Tacoma, Washington. There wasn't a cloud in the sky. All of the sudden, I heard an unexpected loud noise. Before I could gain my senses, a stealth bomber appeared out of the blue. It is a moment that I will never forget! In a similar way, wolves literally appear out of nowhere. They are not easily detected. They are engaged in covert activities at the bidding of their father, the devil. These wolves are stealthy.

Acts 20:29-30 reveal three specific ways that wolves showcase this stealthy behavior. Verse 29 suggests that that when strong, godly leaders depart, deceivers step in: "I know that after my departure fierce wolves will come in among you ..." In the early church, the wolves knew that the apostle Paul had a passion for church planting. So once Paul was gone, they would have a better chance of infiltrating the church with their lies, treachery, and deceit.

Verse 29 reveals the origin of these wolves. Surprisingly, they "come in among you." In many cases, the wolves come from inside the household of faith. These wolves are not only stealthy; they are smart, cunning, and sly. They are theological spymasters who carefully worm their way into local churches and even make their way into leadership circles, including elder councils and deacon boards.

Paul continues in verse 30: " ... and from among your own selves will arise men speaking twisted things, to draw away the disciples after them." The word translated *arise* means "to spring up and rebel against." These wolves are like clandestine operatives who infiltrate enemy territory. They gain all the intelligence they need until one day they rise up and create an unholy cacophony in the church.

Next, *wolves are relentless.* Paul says, "they will not spare the flock." The Greek word translated *not sparing* (*mēpheidomai*) means "to refrain from harming." The term is written in the present tense, meaning that the wolves will relentlessly pursue the flock. Like a real-life voracious wolf, these beasts are on a mission to devour the sheep. They seek to deceive the sheep. They will intimidate the sheep and strike fear in their souls. The aim of these wolves is to bring great harm to the flock of God.

Fourth, *wolves are doctrinal deceivers.* The Phillips paraphrase of Acts 20:30 is revealing: "Yes, and even among you men will arise speaking perversions of the truth." The English Standard Version says, " ... and from among your own selves will arise men speaking twisted things, to draw away the disciples after them." The phrase *speaking twisted things* means, "to pervert or bend the truth." Such a person twists the truth in order to deceive the people of God and lead them away from truth and ultimately lead them away from God. Notice how Paul alerts the church to these doctrinal deceivers in the following passages:

> *Certain persons, by swerving from these, have wandered away into vain discussion, desiring to be teachers of the law, without understanding either what they are saying or the things about which they make confident assertions (1 Tim. 1:6-7).*

> *You are aware that all who are in Asia turned away from me, among whom are Phygelus and Hermogenes (2 Tim. 1:15).*

> *... And their talk will spread like gangrene. Among them are Hymenaeus and Philetus, who have swerved from the truth, saying that the resurrection has already happened. They are upsetting the faith of some (2 Tim. 2:17-18).*

Of course, if gangrene goes untreated, it will eat the flesh of the infected patient and ultimately result in death. Such is the fate of a church that allows the doctrinal deception of wolves to infiltrate their ranks.

I can think of a handful of friends over the years who have been deceived by theological wolves. These ferocious beasts relentlessly pursued my friends and led them down a path of personal and doctrinal destruction. Some of these people were lured in by wolves and never seen again.

Fifth, wolves are *spiritual kidnappers.* Acts 20:30 tells us that the wolves aim is to "draw away the disciples after them." *Draw* comes from a Greek word that means "to change someone's beliefs through deceptive means or cause a person to be attracted to beliefs." The term actually means "to tear away." Wolves work with all their might to tear professing followers of Christ from the fold of God.

One of the clearest examples of this kind of deceit is in the theology of Charles G. Finney. Revered by many as a great evangelist and revivalist preacher, Finney rejected the doctrine of justification by faith and the doctrine of original sin. He held that sinners have a natural ability to obey God. He insisted that depravity was a voluntary condition and believed that sinners have the power simply to will otherwise. He believed that sin results from wrong choices, not from a fallen nature. Phil Johnson notes, "According to Finney, sinners can freely reform their hearts, and must do so themselves if they are to be redeemed."[17] Additionally, Finney repudiated the doctrine of penal substitutionary atonement. Charles G. Finney was a modern day Pelagian. Yet, he is still held in high esteem by many evangelicals. If a man like Finney can influence evangelicals, how much more can the theological wolves of our day ravage the church?

PREACHING IN THE SHADOW OF LENIN

I was recently reminded of the grim reality of the fear factor as I walked by a massive statute of Vladimir Lenin in one of the former Soviet Republics. The daunting image of the tyrannical leader of the Soviet Union cast a glance in my direction as I made my way to a local church. My task that day was to faithfully preach the Word of God to a group of Christ-followers. Even after the collapse of the Soviet Union, a trickle of fear ran up and down my spine. A man who died almost a hundred years ago still caused fear to rise within my soul.

Contending with wolves is one of the many threats that face the contemporary church. The reason for courage and conviction becomes apparent as we consider this ominous threat. Later, we will present a strategy for protecting the sheep, which is grounded in biblical principles of courage. But first, we must turn to part two: *the recovery of courage.*

---

[17] Phillip R. Johnson, *A Wolf in Sheep's Clothing: How Charles Finney's Theology Ravaged the Evangelical Movement*, 1998.

PART 2

THE RECOVERY OF
COURAGE AND CONVICTION

*"Be of good comfort, Master Ridley, and play the man;
we shall this day, by God's grace, light such a candle in
England as I trust shall never be put out."*

Hugh Latimer

⇒ 3 ⇐

A SUPERCHARGED PRAYER
FOR COURAGE AND CONVICTION

———— ••• ————

"The world always respects those most who act boldly for God. Oh, break these bonds, and cast these chains from you! Never be ashamed of letting these men see you want to go to heaven. Think it no disgrace to show yourself a servant of God. Never be afraid of doing what is right."[18]

J.C. Ryle

The recovery of courage and conviction begins in an unlikely place. A Christian who is characterized by courage and conviction must first make a commitment to being a man or woman of humility. Such a decision is counterintuitive in our culture. The same was true among the Greeks. The Greeks maintained that meekness was tantamount to weakness. Lloyd-Jones reminds us that meekness was simply non-existent in Greek culture: "There was no word for meekness in Greek pagan philosophy. Courage, and strength, and power—those were the things they believed in ... They placed no value on meekness and on humility; courage and power and heroism were the great virtues."[19]

---

[18] J.C. Ryle, *Thoughts for Young Men* (Louisville: GLH Publishing, 2017), Loc. 367.

[19] Martyn Lloyd-Jones, *God's Way of Reconciliation: An Exposition of Ephesians 2* (Grand Rapids: Baker Book House, 1972), 64.

So when we speak of recovering courage and conviction, we are faced with a unique dilemma. Our culture is similar to the ancient Greeks. We tend to admire the courageous. We exalt the brave. And we applaud the powerful. But we also have a tendency to despise the humble person; the one who puts others first; the one who considers others before himself. But authentic courage and conviction is grounded in biblical humility. "But this is the one to whom I will look: he who is humble and contrite in spirit and trembles at my word" (Isa. 66:2b). Authentic courage is grounded in a meek and humble spirit that trusts God by clinging to his Word.

Christians committed to a life of humility, then, need consistent encouragement. Anyone who minimizes the importance of encouragement is disconnected from reality. Church history is filled with examples of people who were in desperate need of encouragement. An example of such a man is Anselm. "I pray, O God, that I may know you and love you, so that I may rejoice in you."[20] Why would Anselm, a godly man, pray like this? I think we can draw an important lesson from this very insightful prayer. The lesson is this: Even the most mature believers have moments of doubt and discouragement. It is not unusual for godly people to experience seasons of spiritual numbness. Spurgeon recounts his battle with depression. Luther and William Cowper do the same. And so Anslem cries out, "I pray, O God, that I may know you and love you, so that I may rejoice in you."

The apostle Paul understands the fragility of the human spirit. In fact, he would have been deeply sympathetic to the nineteenth century tune, which offers this sobering lament:

Prone to wander, Lord I feel it, prone to leave the God I love; Here's my heart, O take and seal it, Seal it for Thy courts above.

King David could have easily penned those words. Jonah lived those words. Peter actually denied the Lord three times!

[20] Anselm, *Proslogion*, Chapter 26. Cited in John Piper, *When I Don't Desire God* (Wheaton: Crossway Books, 2004), 136.

You and I could have easily written those words—because each of us experience the grinding challenges of the Christian life on a regular basis. And so there is a real possibility of wandering for a season in a spiritual wasteland. The prospect of growing depressed, discouraged or battling unbelief is something that each of us face.[21] Indeed, this is a daily reality that we must contend with. Spurgeon says, "I am the subject of depression of spirit so fearful that I hope none of you ever get to such extremes of wretchedness as I go to."[22] "Spiritual sorrows," says Spurgeon, "are the worst of mental miseries."[23]

What about you? Where does God need to give you courage?

- Courage to live the Christian life?

- Courage to flee from temptation?

- Courage to boldly proclaim the truth?

- Courage to boldly defend the faith?

- Courage to remain resolute in the face of adversity?

Paul understands that his friends in Ephesus, like us, need Christian courage. We need constant encouragement as fallen creatures. And so he prays for them. He prays for us:

> *For this reason I bow my knees before the Father, from whom every family in heaven and on earth is named, that according to the riches of his glory he may grant you to be strengthened with power through his Spirit in your inner being, so that Christ may dwell in your hearts through faith—that you, being rooted and grounded in love, may have strength to comprehend with all the saints what is the breadth and length and height and depth, and to know*

[21] See Barnabas Piper, *Help My Unbelief: Why Doubt is Not the Enemy of Faith* (Epsom: United Kingdom, 2020).

[22] Charles Spurgeon, "Joy and Peace in Believing," *Metropolitan Tabernacle Pulpit*, Vol., 12, Sermon 692 (http://www.spurgeongems.org/vols 10-12/chs692.pdf). Cited in Zach Eswine, *Spurgeon's Sorrows* (Geanies House: Christian Focus Publications, 2014), 13.

[23] Charles Spurgeon, "Lama Sabachthani?" MTP, vol. 36 (Ages Digital Library, 1998), 168. Cited in Ibid.

the love of Christ that surpasses knowledge, that you may be filled with all the fullness of God. Now to him who is able to do far more abundantly than all that we ask or think, according to the power at work within us, to him be glory in the church and in Christ Jesus throughout all generations, forever and ever. Amen (Eph. 3:14–21).

THE FRAMEWORK OF PAUL'S PRAYER

The Priority of Prayer

Immediately after unpacking the drama of the gospel, Paul prays for the people of God (v. 14). Since he understands their propensity to wander and get off track, he commits them to God. Throughout his ministry, we find Paul praying for people.

- He prayed for the Corinthians (2 Cor. 13:7, 9).
- He prayed for the Colossians (Col. 1:3, 9).
- He prayed for the Thessalonians (1 Thess. 3:10; 2 Thess. 1:11).
- He prayed for the Philippians (Phil. 1:9).
- He prayed for the Romans (Rom. 12:12).

The priority of prayer was at the very heart of Paul's ministry. Such a ministry fueled the courage of the Ephesian believers. This priority of prayer should stand at the center of our lives and ministries as well.

The Posture of Prayer

Paul assumes a posture of prayer that displays humility. He remembers who he is by getting on his knees. The best possible place for the people of God is on their knees. *Bow* (ESV) and *kneel* (CSB) come from the Greek term *kámptō*, which means "to worship." When he assumes the proper posture, he begins to pour out his heart on behalf of his friends in Ephesus, not to mention all subsequent believers: "For this reason I bow my knees before the Father, from whom every family in heaven and on earth is named ..." (Eph. 3:14–15). "Whether we actually bow our knees," writes Warren Wiersbe, "is not the important thing; that we bow our hearts and wills to the Lord and ask Him for what we need is a vital matter."[24] Simply put, God is drawn to the humble man (Eph. 3:14; c.f. Jas. 4:6-10; Isa. 66:2). C.J. Mahaney adds, "Humility draws the gaze of our sovereign God ... God is personally and providentially supportive of the humble."[25]

The Pattern of Prayer

Additionally, Paul addresses God the Father. While each member of the Trinity is fully God, the apostle understands (as Jesus taught in Matthew 6:9) that our prayer is directed to the Father, through (or in the name of the Son), in the power of the Spirit. Bruce A. Ware observes, "The Father, then, as supreme authority over even his own Son and the Spirit, is the one to whom we gladly but humbly address our prayers."[26] We realize that a proper understanding of the Trinity becomes an important theological reality as we grow in our understanding of prayer and the pursuit of God.

THE FOCUS OF PAUL'S PRAYER

Paul continues his prayer:

> ... that according to the riches of his glory he may grant you to be strengthened with power through his Spirit in your inner being, so that Christ may dwell in your hearts through faith—that you, being rooted and grounded in love, may have strength to comprehend with all the saints what is the breadth and length and height and depth, and to know the love of Christ that surpasses knowledge, that you may be filled with all the fullness of God (Eph. 3:16–19).

---

[24] Warren Wiersbe, *The Bible Exposition Commentary* (Vol. 2, p. 31). Wheaton: Victor Books, 1996).

[25] C.J. Mahaney, *Humility: True Greatness* (Sisters: Multnomah Publishers, 2005), 19, 21.

[26] Bruce A. Ware, *Father, Son, and Holy Spirit: Relationships, Roles, and Relevance* (Wheaton: Crossway Books, 2005), 152.

In order to understand the basis of this prayer, we need to familiarize ourselves with a biblical term which is regularly applied to God. The term that I am referring to is *glory* (v. 16). The Greek term *dóxa*, which is translated *glory*, means "splendor, brightness or honor." It signifies "gravity" or "greatness." Therefore, glory implies praise!

> *And as soon as Aaron spoke to the whole congregation of the people of Israel, they looked toward the wilderness, and behold, the glory of the LORD appeared in the cloud (Exod. 16:10).*

> *The glory of the LORD dwelt on Mount Sinai, and the cloud covered it six days. And on the seventh day he called to Moses out of the midst of the cloud (Exod. 24:16).*

> *Now the appearance of the glory of the LORD was like a devouring fire on the top of the mountain in the sight of the people of Israel (Exod. 24:17).*

> *Moses said, 'Please show me your glory' (Exod. 33:18).*

> *... and while my glory passes by I will put you in a cleft of the rock, and I will cover you with my hand until I have passed by (Exod. 33:22).*

> *Then the cloud covered the tent of meeting, and the glory of the LORD filled the tabernacle (Exod. 40:34).*

> *But truly, as I live, and as all the earth shall be filled with the glory of the LORD, (Numb. 14:21).*

> *Then Moses and Aaron went from the presence of the assembly to the entrance of the tent of meeting and fell on their faces. And the glory of the LORD appeared to them, (Numb. 20:6).*

> *Ascribe to the LORD, O families of the peoples, ascribe to the LORD glory and strength! (1 Chron. 16:28).*

> *Yours, O LORD, is the greatness and the power and the glory and the victory and the majesty, for all that is in the heavens and in the earth is yours. Yours is the kingdom, O LORD, and you are exalted as head above all (1 Chron. 29:11).*

O LORD, our Lord, how majestic is your name in all the earth! You have set your glory above the heavens (Ps. 8:1).

Who is this King of glory? The LORD, strong and mighty, the LORD, mighty in battle! (Ps. 24:8).

Ascribe to the LORD the glory due his name; worship the LORD in the splendor of holiness (Ps. 29:2).

The focus of Paul's prayer finds its basis in the "riches" of God's glory. *Riches (ploûtos)* means "abundant wealth." In other words, Paul's request to the Father is according to the super-abounding treasure chest of God. Each of these prayer requests, then, flow from the never-ending bounty or treasure chest of God's glory!

Courage to Live for God

To live courageously means to demonstrate "mental or moral strength to persevere and withstand danger, fear, or difficulty."[27] So the essence of this first request is a prayer for *supernatural power.* This power *(dunamis)* is "ability" or "supernatural power." Paul prays, "… that according to the riches of his glory he may grant you to be strengthened with power through his Spirit in your inner being" (Eph. 3:16).

This spiritual strength is to be received through the Holy Spirit in the "inner being." That is, the Holy Spirit is bestowed in the inner man. Jesus promises this supernatural power to the disciples. He says, "But you will receive power when the Holy Spirit has come upon your and you will be my witnesses in Jerusalem and in all Judea and Samaria, and to the end of the earth" (Acts 1:8). Therefore, the Holy Spirit is our means of spiritual strength. He is the divine Agent behind the courage that Paul prays for. Think carefully for a moment about the ministry of the Holy Spirit:

- The Holy Spirit is the third member of the Trinity.

- The Holy Spirit is co-equal and co-eternal with the Father and the Son.

- The Holy Spirit raised Jesus from the dead (Rom. 8:11).

[27] https//www.merriam-webster.copm/dictionary/courage.

- The Holy Spirit empowered Jesus to withstand temptation in the wilderness (Luke 4:1).

- The Holy Spirit moved the hearts and the minds of the authors of Scripture. Bruce Ware adds, "They wrote the truths that were on their hearts, with the words, grammar, and syntax that they chose to use—the Spirit was working in them so that what they wrote was simultaneously their word and God's Word."[28]

- It is the Holy Spirit who wakes people who are dead in sin and regenerates their sinful hearts (John 3:3-8; Eph. 2:1; Acts 26:18). It is the Spirit who conforms us to the image of Christ (2 Cor. 3:18). It is "through the Spirit," Paul says, that we will be strengthened with power "so that Christ may dwell in your hearts through faith" (Eph. 3:16-17). We desperately need this spiritual strength from God because:

- It is the Spirit who conforms us to the image of Christ (2 Cor. 3:18).

It is "through the Spirit," Paul says, that we will be strengthened with power "so that Christ may dwell in your hearts through faith" (Eph. 3:16-17). We desperately need this spiritual strength from God because:

- Apart from divine strength, we are weak (2 Cor. 12:29).

- Apart from divine strength, we are inclined to give up (2 Cor. 1:8-9).

- Apart from divine strength, we succumb to discouragement, fear, and anxiety (2 Cor. 11:28).

- Apart from divine strength, we are inclined to sin (Rom. 7:15-20).

When we are courageous, our perspective gets recalibrated and rejuvenated. When we are courageous, we are reminded that " ... we are more than conquerors through him who loved us. For I am sure that neither death nor life, nor angels nor rulers, nor

---

[28] Bruce A. Ware, *Father, Son, and Holy Spirit,* 108.

things present nor things to come, nor powers, nor height nor depth, nor anything else in all creation, will be able to separate us from the love of God in Christ Jesus our Lord" (Rom. 8:37-39). Thank God for this prayer that brings spiritual strength and renews the people of God!

Comprehending the Character of God

The second request concerns spiritual understanding. *Comprehend* (katalambànō) means "to lay hold of; to grasp with the intellect." Paul's prayer is that the Ephesian believers would have the strength to intellectually grasp with all the saints what is the breadth and length and height and depth of God.

The Westminster Shorter Catechism sheds light on this important matter:

> *Q: What is God?*
>
> *A: God is spirit, infinite, eternal, and unchangeable in his being, wisdom, power, holiness, justice, goodness, and truth.*

Paul's prayer is that the Ephesians and every subsequent Christian would *comprehend* who God is. Please understand this great mystery—we will never fully comprehend God. I can vividly remember one of my Seminary professors stressing this very point. Since God is eternal, we will never understand God comprehensively. Indeed, we will grow in our knowledge of God unto all eternity! Wayne Grudem adds, "Because God is infinite and we are finite or limited, we can never fully understand God … Even though we cannot know God exhaustively, we can know *true* things about God."[29] The Scriptures emphasize this truth again and again:

> *Great is the Lord, and abundant in prayer; his understanding is beyond measure (Ps. 147:5).*
>
> *Oh, the depth of the riches and wisdom and knowledge of God! How unsearchable are his judgments and how inscrutable are his ways! (Rom. 11:33).*

---

[29] Wayne Grudem, *Systematic Theology* (Grand Rapids: Zondervan, 1994), 149, 151.

Paul's prayer is that we would *comprehend* the God of Psalm 8:1-9:

O LORD, our Lord, how majestic is your name in all the earth! You have set your glory above the heavens. Out of the mouth of babies and infants, you have established strength because of your foes, to still the enemy and the avenger. When I look at your heavens, the work of your fingers, the moon and the stars, which you have set in place, what is man that you are mindful of him, and the son of man that you care for him? Yet you have made him a little lower than the heavenly beings and crowned him with glory and honor. You have given him dominion over the works of your hands; you have put all things under his feet, all sheep and oxen, and also the beasts of the field, the birds of the heavens, and the fish of the sea, whatever passes along the paths of the seas. O LORD, our Lord, how majestic is your name in all the earth!

Paul's prayer is that we would *comprehend* the God of Isaiah 40:10-14:

Behold, the Lord GOD comes with might, and his arm rules for him; behold, his reward is with him, and his recompense before him. He will tend his flock like a shepherd; he will gather the lambs in his arms; he will carry them in his bosom, and gently lead those that are with young. Who has measured the waters in the hollow of his hand and marked off the heavens with a span, enclosed the dust of the earth in a measure and weighed the mountains in scales and the hills in a balance? Who has measured the Spirit of the LORD, or what man shows him his counsel? Whom did he consult, and who made him understand? Who taught him the path of justice, and taught him knowledge, and showed him the way of understanding? Behold, the nations are like a drop from a bucket, and are accounted as the dust on the scales; behold, he takes up the coastlands like fine dust.

Paul's prayer is that we would *comprehend* the God of 1 Chronicles 29:11:

Yours, O LORD, is the greatness and the power and the glory and the victory and the majesty, for all that is in the heavens and in the earth is yours. Yours is the kingdom, O

LORD, and you are exalted as head above all.

Paul's prayer is that we would *comprehend* the God of Exodus 15:11:

> *Who is like you, O LORD, among the gods? Who is like you, majestic in holiness, awesome in glorious deeds, doing wonders?*

Pauls' prayer is that we would *comprehend* the God of Revelation 19:11-16:

> *Then I saw heaven opened, and behold, a white horse! The one sitting on it is called Faithful and True, and in righteousness he judges and makes war. His eyes are like a flame of fire, and on his head are many diadems, and he has a name written that no one knows but himself. He is clothed in a robe dipped in blood, and the name by which he is called is The Word of God. And the armies of heaven, arrayed in fine linen, white and pure, were following him on white horses. From his mouth comes a sharp sword with which to strike down the nations, and he will rule them with a rod of iron. He will tread the winepress of the fury of the wrath of God the Almighty. On his robe and on his thigh he has a name written, King of kings and Lord of lords.*

Are you wondering how this prayer will be answered? Verse 17 tells us: We grow in our understanding of who God is by being "rooted and grounded in love." *Rooted (*ridsòō*)* is a term that means "to be established; to be fixed into the ground." Paul calls believers to be rooted and built up in Christ and established in the faith (Col. 2:7). *Grounded (*themelióō) means "to lay a foundation; to establish belief, or be strengthened." Paul reveals the magnificent result in verses 18-19 namely, that we might have a supernatural understanding of the greatness of God and be filled with "all the fullness of God."

Three Ways to Get Grounded in Christ

Paul's request for the Ephesian believers and every subsequent Christian is unmistakable. Therefore, we must take practical steps to get firmly grounded in Christ. At least three practical steps will help us move forward in the right direction.

First, *get to know the Bible*. Sit under the faithful ministry of pastors and teachers who provide accurate exposition and fresh insight from Scripture (Rom. 10:17). *Read* the Word of God. This habit gives us an overview of the Bible and becomes the crucial foundation with which to live our Christian lives (Rev. 1:3). *Study* the Word of God, which deepens theological convictions (Acts 17:11). *Memorize* the Word of God, which enables us to use the Sword of the Spirit to overcome temptation and have verses prepared for ministering to people and evangelizing them. *Meditate* on the Word of God. The psalmist writes, "Blessed is the man who walks not in the counsel of the wicked, nor stands in the way of sinners, nor sits in the seat of scoffers; but his delight is in the law of the LORD, and on his law he meditates day and night. He is like a tree planted by streams of water that yields its fruit in its season, and its leaf does not wither. In all that he does, he prospers" (Psalm 1:1–3). Getting to know the Bible will embolden us and grant courage to withstand every challenge and obstacle. Becoming familiar with Scripture will help us weather the difficult seasons that each of us will face.

Second, *get comfortable with systematic theology*. Outside of reading Scripture, nothing has helped me more than studying systematic theology. These outstanding resources are readily accessible and will prove to be a great encouragement in your Christian life. I recommend beginning with Wayne Grudem's, *Systematic Theology: An Introduction to Bible Doctrine*. But don't stop with Grudem's work. Commit to working your way through John Frame's, *Systematic Theology: An Introduction to Christian Belief*, and John MacArthur's, *Biblical Doctrine: A Systematic Summary of Bible Truth*. But don't stop with these current writers. Make an effort to read some of the great thinkers of the Christian faith. Study through the three-volume set, *Systematic Theology* by Charles Hodge. Work through *Systematic Theology* by Louis Berkof. Read John Calvin's *Institutes of the Christian*

Religion. And pour over the heart-warming words by Herman Bavnick in his *Reformed Dogmatics.*

Third, *get familiar with the attributes of God.* I am convinced that large numbers of Christians are neglecting the biblical portrait of God. More than ever, professing Christians are creating a "god" of their own making. For example, Joel Osteen says, "It doesn't matter who likes you or doesn't like you, all that matters is God likes you. He accepts you, he approves of you."[30] Instead of embracing the biblical portrait of God that we find in the Scripture, sinful people are creating a god in their imaginations. A.W. Pink makes this sobering lament: "How vastly different is the God of Scripture from the 'god of the average pulpit."[31] Tozer continues, "So necessary to the Church is a lofty concept of God that when that concept in any measure declines, the Church with her worship and her moral standards declines along with it. The first step down for any church is taken when it surrenders its high opinion of God."[32] A few months ago, I read an article that demonstrates the reality of Tozer's "slippery slope." The piece told that sad story of a church that decided to adopt a new "non-discrimination policy" that would allow same-sex marriage ceremonies, membership, leadership positions, church ordinances, and ordination to openly gay and transgender individuals without telling them their lifestyles contradict biblical teaching."

How could such a thing happen? How did a church who historically affirmed the authority, inspiration, inerrancy, and veracity of Scripture reach this point? No doubt, there were many factors that led to their new policy. But the reality is this: They compromised their view of God and his Word. They joined the ranks of the spineless!

---

[30] Joel Osteen, cited in Shana Raley-Lusk, Joel Osteen Controversial Quotes, 8 May, 2015.

[31] A.W. Pink, *The Attributes of God* (Grand Rapids: Baker Book House, 1975), 11.

[32] Ibid, 10.

Three important principles guide our thinking and guard our Christian worldview when it comes to our approach to God. Let's refer to these as the A,B,C's of theology:

1. Always distinguish between the Creator and the creature. A.W. Tozer reminds us, "To think of creature and Creator alike in essential being is to rob God of most of His attributes and reduce Him to the status of a creature. It is, for instance to rob Him of His infinitude: there cannot be two unlimited substances in the universe. It is to take away His sovereignty: there cannot be two absolutely free beings in the universe, for sooner or later two completely free wills must collide."[33]

2. Banish idolatrous thoughts of God. Calvin warned readers in the sixteenth-century about their propensity to create false gods: "Hence we may infer, that the human mind is, so to speak, a perpetual forge of idols ... The human mind, stuffed as it is with presumptuous rashness, dares to imagine a God suited to its own capacity; as it labors under dullness, no, is sunk in the grossest ignorance, it substitutes vanity and an empty phantom in the place of God."[34] Scripture argues strenuously, "You shall have no other gods before me. You shall not make for yourself a carved image, or any likeness of anything that is in heaven above, or that is in the earth beneath, or that is in the water under the earth. You shall not bow down to them or serve them, for I the LORD your God am a jealous God, visiting the iniquity of the fathers on the children to the third and the fourth generation of those who hate me, but showing steadfast love to thousands of those who love me and keep my commandments" (Exod. 20:3-6).

3. Commit to thinking biblically about God. I believe that the greatest issue facing the church in any century is a

---

[33] Ibid, 8.

[34] John Calvin, *Institutes of the Christian Religion* (Peabody: Hendrickson Publishers, 2008), 55

proper understanding of who God is. We need a steady diet of the attributes and perfections of God. A high and robust doctrine of God will breed a worshiping congregation. We must commit to thinking rightly about God because this influences everything else in life. If we ever hope to worship God rightly, our view of God must always be reforming, which involves constantly remolding, recalibrating, and reviving our vision of God.[35]

Communion with God

Paul's final request is communion with God (Eph. 3:19). This is a plea for relational intimacy. *Know (ginōskō)* refers to "experiential knowledge." The apostle's prayer in Philippians 3:10 is that he would know (Christ) "and the power of his resurrection, and may share his sufferings, becoming like him in his death" (Phil. 3:10). This is the kind of knowledge that makes its home in both the head and the heart. Paul prays that the Ephesian believers would *know* the love of Christ that surpasses knowledge, which goes beyond a basic understanding. His prayer is that the Ephesians would enjoy vital communion with God! The Puritan divine, John Owen, unpacks the essential nature of this Christ-exalting communion:

> You do not hold communion with God in anything until you receive it by faith ... You will never experience the sweetness of his love until you receive it. You must, then, continually remind yourself that God loves you and embraces you with his free eternal love. When the Lord is, by his Word, presented as a Father who loves you, then think about it and accept it. Then embrace him by faith and let your heart be filled with his love. Set your whole heart to receive his love and let your heart be bound with the cords of this love.[36]

---

[35] The Reformers were fond of saying, "*Ecclesia reformat, temper reformanda,*" meaning *"the church reformed, always reforming."*

[36] John Owen, *Communion with God* (Edinburgh: Banner of Truth Trust, 1991), 30.

This relational intimacy also means that we will be filled with all the fullness of God. *Fullness (pleirōma)* means "completeness of full measure." This is the depth of the communion of God that Paul prays that the Ephesian believers would receive. This is the kind of communion with God that we should enjoy on a daily basis.

I do not know of any Christian who would turn down the opportunity to receive spiritual strength (courage), spiritual understanding (comprehension), and spiritual communion. These are not empty requests. These are not mere words on a page. These are requests that Paul anticipates becoming a reality.

Notice Paul's triumphant conclusion: "Now to him who is able to do far more abundantly than all that we ask or think, according to the power at work within us, to him be glory in the church and in Christ Jesus throughout all generations, forever and ever. Amen" (Eph. 3:20-21).

J.C. Ryle adds:

Strive to live a courageous life. Confess Christ before men. Whatever station you occupy, in that station confess Christ. Why should you be ashamed of him? He was not ashamed of you on the cross. He is ready to confess you now before his Father in heaven. Why should you be ashamed of him? Be bold. Be very bold. The good soldier is not ashamed of his uniform. The true believer ought never to be ashamed of Christ.[37]

Oh, that the people of God would have courage to live for God, that they would comprehend him through the lens of Scripture, and enjoy unhindered communion with him! What is

[37] J.C. Ryle, *Holiness: Its Nature, Hindrances, Difficulties, and Roots,* 302.

preventing you from this kind of a God-centered life? May the supercharged prayer become a reality for you—"to him be glory in the church and in Christ Jesus throughout all generations, forever and ever. Amen."

⤜ 4 ⤛

A STAUNCH ALLEGIANCE TO THE WORD OF GOD

···

"Cross-bearing always involves cost, especially when undertaking a direct and relentless assault on the gates of hell."[38]

Tim Keesee

The recovery of courage and conviction is dependent upon a rock-solid allegiance to the Word of God. Anything less than a full-orbed and radical commitment to the truth of Scripture will fall short and fail to propel the people of God in a fruitful direction. The stakes are high as the culture militates against biblical authority at every juncture. Anyone who dares to uphold God's Word is bound to be mocked and ridiculed. But the people of God must stand up and boldly proclaim the truth of Scripture. They must maintain their resolve in the face of adversity. The first step to recovering courage and conviction is a staunch allegiance to the Word of God.

THE TIPPING POINT

Acts 5:27-29 tells a story about a group of men who refused to compromise their convictions. Here we find the high priest and Sadducees filled with jealousy, which led to the arrest of the apostles (vv. 17-18). In the middle of the night, an angel of the

---

[38] Tim Keesee, *A Company of Heroes: Portraits from the Gospel's Global Advance* (Wheaton: Crossway Books, 2019), 256.

Lord rescued them from the confines of prison and instructed them, "Go and stand in the temple and speak to the people all the words of this Life" (v. 20). At the break of dawn, they made their way to the temple and taught the word of God (v. 21). When the high priest summoned the officials to bring the apostles forward, they learned that they had escaped and were teaching the people. Notice how the story plays out:

> *And when they had brought them, they set them before the council. And the high priest questioned them, saying, 'We strictly charged you not to teach in this name, yet here you have filled Jerusalem with your teaching, and you intend to bring this man's blood upon us.' But Peter and the apostles answered, 'We must obey God rather than men' (Acts 5:27–29).*

God is looking for men and women of conviction. He expects each of us to be men and women of unshakeable and unwavering conviction. Exactly what fueled the convictions of Peter and the apostles in Acts 5? What were the contours of their convictions? From where did they gain such unbelievable courage? The answer to these questions will help fuel our resolve and shore up our convictions and courage in the Christian life.

While several contributing factors fueled the apostles' convictions, it was first and foremost their devotion to the Word of God. One can only imagine what was running through the minds of the apostles when they stood before the high priest and council for a second time. They had already been imprisoned for exercising their convictions. So these men do not stand before the council with cavalier attitudes. This is serious business. They understood that their lives were on the line.[39]

Have you ever found yourself in a similar situation? Have you ever stood before your employer with a choice to bear witness to the truth? Have your friends ridiculed you for your commitment to the historic Christian faith? Have you ever paid the price for

---

[39] Notice that after they bear witness to the truth of God's word, the council was "enraged and wanted to kill them" (Acts 5:33).

refusing to compromise your convictions? This is exactly where we find the apostles. But in their case, their lives are literally at stake.

DEVOTION TO THE WORD

The apostles' devotion to the Word fueled their convictions. Notice three unmovable pillars that undergird their steadfast devotion to the Word of God.

The Word is Truth

The apostles did not question the truthfulness of God's Word; they humbled themselves before it. They did not scoff at the truth of the Word; they submitted to it. The apostles did not doubt the truthfulness of God's Word; they were devoted to it. Yet how often do we subject the truth of Scripture to a set of worldly benchmarks? How often do we buy into the postmodern lie that either marginalizes or ridicules propositional truth? For instance, one writer says, "There is no truth; truth is relative to the community in which we participate."[40]

There are only two options before us. We either *repudiate* the truth like Pilate (John 18:38) or we *revere* the truth like Jesus and the apostles. "Then Pilate said to him, 'So you are a king?' Jesus answered, 'You say that I am a king. For this purpose I was born and for this purpose I have come into the world - to bear witness to the truth. Everyone who is of the truth listens to my voice'" (John 18:37; c.f. John 17:17).

The council said to the apostles, "We strictly charged you not to teach in this name, yet here you have filled Jerusalem with your teaching, and you intend to bring this man's blood upon us" (Acts 5:28). But the apostles were devoted to the Word of God. They believed in the truthfulness of the Word. They refused to take the spineless path.

---

[40] Cited in Stanley Grenz, *A Primer on Postmodernism* (Grand Rapids: Eerdmans Publishing Company, 1996), 8. Jean-François Lyotard defined postmodernism as "incredulity about metanarratives." See Millard Erickson, *Truth or Consequences* (Downers Grove: IVP, 2001), 15.

One man in church history was literally on fire for the truth. The day was February 4, 1555. The man roped to the pyre was known well in the British village - a man of humble origins; a man of bold ambitions and a simple obedience to match. This man dared to challenge the throne with two basic acts - preaching the Word of God and printing the Matthews-Tyndale Bible. His name was John Rogers - pastor, father, martyr. He was the first Christian to pay the ultimate price of death during Mary Tudor's bloody reign of terror overtook the British countryside. He was the first of hundreds who would die at the hands of this blood-thirsty tyrant.

Like John Rogers, the apostles believed in the truthfulness of God's Word. "So come what will," they said. "Accuse us, mock us, ridicule us, scorn us, or kill us. We believe in and we preach the absolute truth of the Bible." While Nietzsche quipped, "Facts do not exist, only interpretations,"[41] the apostles embraced the facts which are clearly spelled out in God's Word.

The French believers, better known as the Huguenots, were persecuted for their unyielding conviction concerning the truth of God's Word. There is an inscription on a monument in Paris that demonstrates their Christian courage in vivid terms: "Hammer away, ye hostile hands; your hammers break; God's anvil stands." We do well to follow in their footsteps.

The Word is Powerful

Peter and the apostles were bold in their stance and unwavering in their resolve: "We must obey God rather than men" (Acts 5:29). How could they say such a thing in the midst of such fiery adversity? The answer is both clear and compelling. They believed that the Word of God is powerful. Scripture declares:

For the word of God is living and active, sharper than any two-edged sword, piercing to the division of soul and spirit, of joints and of marrow, and discerning the thoughts

---

[41] Friedrich Nietzsche, *The Portable Nietzsche*, 458. Cited in Nancy Pearcey, *Love Thy Body* (Grand Rapids: Baker, 2018), 165.

and intentions of the heart (Heb. 4:12).

Is not my word like fire, declares the LORD, and like a hammer that breaks the rock in pieces? (Jer. 23:29).

Martin Luther believed in the power of the Word: "I simply taught, preached, wrote the Word; otherwise I did nothing. And then, while I slept, or drank Wittenberg beer with my Phillip (Melanchthon) and my son (Nicholas von) Amsdorf, the Word so greatly weakened the papacy that never a prince or emperor did such damage to it. I did nothing. The Word did it all."[42] The apostles were able to withstand fiery persecution because they relied on the mighty power of God's Word.

The Word is Authoritative

Finally, the apostles understood that when the Word speaks, God speaks. Do you want to hear a word from God? Do you want to hear the voice of God? Open your Bible and read it. Stop relying on inward impressions and subjective feelings and open the Book!

When the apostles answered, "We must obey God rather than men, they meant it." The Greek word, *peitharcheō* is translated "obey." The term means "to obey someone in authority." The same word is used in verse 32: "And we are witnesses to these things, and so is the Holy Spirit, whom God has given to those who *obey* him."

The Word of God carries the weight of divine authority. "The authority of Scripture" writes Wayne Grudem, "means that all the words in Scripture are God's words in such a way to disbelieve or disobey any word of Scripture is to disbelieve or disobey God."[43] The apostles clung tenaciously to the authoritative Word. When you believe in and embrace the authoritative Word of God, it fuels your convictions. When you bank on the

---

[42] Martin Luther, cited in Timothy George, *Theology of the Reformers* (Nashville: B&H, 2013), 54.

[43] Wayne Grudem, *Systematic Theology: An Introduction to Biblical Doctrine* (Grand Rapids: Zondervan, 1994), 73.

authority of Scripture, it kindles your courage. This is the effect that the authoritative Word had on the apostles.

The apostles' devotion to the Word of God fueled their convictions and kindled their courage. The Word is *truth*. The Word is *powerful*. The Word is *authoritative*. These were the unshakeable pillars that fortified their worldview and enabled them to stand resolute, even in the midst of fiery persecution. Our challenge, then, is to model the strength of their convictions and emulate their Christian courage.

J.C. Ryle's critique of the 19th-century jellyfish is as relevant now as it was almost two hundred years ago:

> *We have myriads of respectable church-going people, who have no distinct and definite views about any point of theology. They cannot discern things that differ, any more than color-blind people can distinguish colors. They think everybody is right—and nobody is wrong. Everything is true and nothing is false. All sermons are good - and none are bad, every clergyman is sound—and no clergyman is unsound.*[44]

When I think about conviction, I am drawn once again to the signers of the *Declaration of Independence*. The men who signed that famed document knew exactly what they were doing. To sign such a document was to declare themselves traitors of the King. If caught, their fate would be sealed. They would surely hang from the gallows.

Stephen Hopkins, one of the signatories of the *Declaration of Independence* was fully aware of the consequences of attaching his name to this historic document. Hopkins, upon signing the document, who suffered from involuntary tremors is said to have remarked, "My hand trembles, but my heart does not."[45] If a man like Stephen Hopkins can muster that kind of resolve in order to gain political freedom, how much more should we be resolute in

---

[44] J.C. Ryle, *Principles for Churchmen* (London: William Hunt, 8 1084), 97-98. Cited in J.I. Packer, *Faithfulness and Holiness*, 72-73.

[45] Cited in David McCullough, *The Course of Human Events* (New York: Simon & Schuster, 2003), Loc. 79.

our biblical convictions? If such a man can demonstrate courage in the face of political persecution, how much more should we stand strong in the Christian life?

COURAGE AND CONVICTION UNLEASHED

God is looking for men and women who say what they mean and mean what they say. He is looking for courageous men and women who let their "yes" be "yes" and their "no" be "no." He is looking for business people who make honest decisions that honor his holy name. He is looking for attorneys who defend the weak and marginalized and ensure that justice is carried out. He's looking for educators who challenge the mind and equip hands and feet that make a difference in the world for God's glory. He's looking for health care providers who protect the unborn and treat people with respect and dignity.

God is looking for preachers who stand tall in the pulpit and refuse to flinch; preachers who proclaim the unadulterated, undiluted Word of God; preachers who refuse to capitulate; preachers who refuse to bow down to the spirit of the age; preachers who insist on bowing down to One person and One person alone—the Lord Jesus Christ!

So farewell to spineless "Christianity." May the next generation of pastors and Christian leaders work together to restore biblical courage and conviction in the people of God.

A STEADFAST COMMITMENT TO PROCLAIM THE TRUTH

———— ••• ————

"O brethren, (he said to his pastors' conference) we shall soon have to die! We look each other in the face to-day in health, but there will come a day when others will look down upon our pallid countenances as we lie in our coffins ... It will matter little to us who shall gaze upon us then, but it will matter eternally how we have discharged our work during our lifetime."[46]

Charles Haddon Spurgeon

Philippians 1:12-18 is a translucent window that gazes deep into the heart of the apostle Paul:

I want you to know, brothers, that what has happened to me has really served to advance the gospel, so that it has become known throughout the whole imperial guard and to all the rest that my imprisonment is for Christ. And most of the brothers, having become confident in the Lord by my imprisonment, are much more bold to speak the word without fear. Some indeed preach Christ from envy and rivalry, but others from good will. The latter do it out of love, knowing that I am put here for the defense of the

[46] Charles Haddon Spurgeon, *An All-Around Ministry*, 76

gospel. The former proclaim Christ out of selfish ambition, not sincerely but thinking to afflict me in my imprisonment. What then? Only that in every way, whether in pretense or in truth, Christ is proclaimed, and in that I rejoice. Yes, and I will rejoice …

FEROCIOUS PERSECUTION

Paul had a staunch commitment to proclaim the truth. His aim was to tell the world about Jesus. Indeed, his passion was to powerfully proclaim the gospel to every person. His commitment helped the gospel spread like wildfire in the ancient world. The gospel would eventually explode in Europe and Africa and China. And the gospel would ignite like wildfire all around the world. What caused the gospel to progress with such great power?

The Method God Used

Imagine serving on a team that is commissioned to help promote the propagation and flourishing of the gospel. What methodology would you employ? Would you initiate a massive advertising campaign? Would you pump money into an evangelism program? Would you enlist an army of volunteers?

In the first-century, God providentially used Paul's imprisonment to cause the powerful spread of the gospel. The persecution came as no surprise to the apostle and should not surprise us either. Jesus told the disciples:

Behold, I am sending you out as sheep in the midst of wolves, so be wise as serpents and innocent as doves. Beware of men, for they will deliver you over to courts and flog you in their synagogues, and you will be dragged before governors and kings for my sake, to bear witness before them and the Gentiles. When they deliver you over, do not be anxious how you are to speak or what you are to say, for what you are to say will be given to you in that hour (Matt. 10:16–19).

One of the methods that God consistently used and continues to use to advance the gospel, then, is persecution.

The Meaning Behind God's Method

Paul refers to the "advance of the gospel." The word *advance* comes from the Greek term, *prokopei*, which refers to "the progress of an army." It comes from a verb that means "to cut down in advance." It describes the removing of any barriers which would hinder the progress of an army. So Paul's imprisonment took place so that the gospel might advance in a mighty and majestic way! The end result is that people would benefit greatly and God would be glorified.

Paul also makes reference to a flourishing gospel, one that became known "throughout the whole imperial guard." "The praetorian guard," writes John MacArthur, was "likely a group of nearly ten thousand soldiers who were stationed throughout Rome to keep the peace and protect the emperor."[47] The apostle glories in this gospel, which became known "to all the rest" for the great name sake of Jesus, his Savior.

The Model Prisoner

The apostle Paul was chained to a Roman guard (Acts 28:16). Consequently, the guards circulated in and out as their shifts changed, which gave Paul a remarkable opportunity to bear witness to Christ. No doubt, the guards would have noticed his body language and learned things about him that would have otherwise been difficult, if not impossible. In short, God used this model prisoner to serve as an ambassador for Christ.

No less than one hundred years later (A.D. 155), Polycarp of Smyrna would also serve as a model prisoner and give up his life for his Savior. After his arrest, the judge ordered Polycarp to renounce his faith in Christ. The judge promised that if he would swear by the emperor and curse Christ, he would be set free. Polycarp's response is priceless: "For eighty-six years I have served him, and he has done me no evil. How could I curse my king, who saved me?"[48] When the judge threatened to burn him in the pyre,

[47] John F. MacArthur, *Philippians* (Chicago: Moody Press, 2001), 61.

[48] Cited in Justo L. Gonzalez, *The Story of Christianity - Vol. 1* (San Francisco: Harper Collins Publishers, 1984), 44.

Polycarp simply answered that "the fire would only last a moment, whereas the eternal fire would never be extinguished." After Polycarp was tied to the post in the pyre, he gazed into the heavens and prayed aloud, "Lord Sovereign God ... I thank you that you deemed me worthy of this moment, so that jointly with your martyrs, I may have a share in the cup of Christ ... I bless and glorify you."[49] The gospel progressed because of ferocious persecution.

Two principles will serve our generation as we seek to fearlessly proclaim the gospel. First, *remember to maintain an eternal perspective*. God providentially permits persecution so that Christ might be proclaimed. We may reason, "In order for the gospel to progress in a country like China, communism must be rooted out." But the reality is this: Communism continues and the underground church is flourishing! God may sovereignly choose to close doors that miraculously open other opportunities. The apostle Paul maintained an eternal perspective. He upheld his passion for the spread of the gospel and made the best of every opportunity.

Second, *allow persecution to strengthen your resolve for proclaiming the gospel of Christ*. When you are ridiculed for believing in a personal Creator who fashioned the world, be encouraged. Continue to proclaim the truth, despite the ferocious persecution. When you are mocked for believing in absolutes, be encouraged that you are challenged for believing that Jesus is the only One who can forgive sin. Continue to proclaim the truth, despite the mocking crowd.

FEARLESS PROCLAMATION

The gospel not only makes progress in the face of ferocious persecution; it strengthens the resolve of Christians to fearlessly proclaim the truth. The Greek term, for *preach* in Philippians 1:15 means "to be a herald; to proclaim with authority." This message must not only be listened to; it must be obeyed. Paul sets forth the imperative to herald the truth:

---

[49] Ibid.

Preach the word; be ready in season and out of season; reprove, rebuke, and exhort, with complete patience and teaching. For the time is coming when people will not endure sound teaching, but having itching ears they will accumulate for themselves teachers to suit their own passions, and will turn away from listening to the truth and wander off into myths (2 Tim. 4:2-4).

Martyn Lloyd-Jones urges, "The most urgent need in the Christian church today is true preaching; and as it is the greatest and most urgent need in the church, it is the greatest need of the world also."[50] Steven Lawson adds, "True biblical preaching is authoritative in nature and boldly proclaims God's Word without compromise or apology."[51] So we endeavor to proclaim the unadulterated truth, courageously and faithfully.

The Defining Marks of Proclamation

Two defining marks of proclamation emerge in Philippians 1:14-17. First, *proclamation must be confident.* The Greek term *peithō*, which is translated as *confident* means "to have faith; to be persuaded of a thing concerning a person—in this case, the Lord Jesus Christ." Scripture highlights the confidence that we enjoy: "For I am sure *(peithō)* that neither death nor life, nor angels nor rulers, nor things present nor things to come, nor powers, nor height nor depth, nor anything else in all creation, will be able to separate us from the love of God in Christ Jesus our Lord" (Rom. 8:38-39).

Second, *proclamation must be bold and fearless.* Paul stresses the importance of speaking the Word boldly and without fear (Phil. 1:14). The word *bold* means "to endure; to have courage." Dr. Luke refers readers to the courage of Paul the apostle who proclaimed the truth "with all boldness and without hindrance" (Acts 28:31). These are the qualities that mark a man who is committed to the proclamation of God's Word.

[50] Martyn Lloyd-Jones, *Preaching and Preachers* (Grand Rapids: Zondervan Publishing House, 1971), 9.

[51] Steven Lawson, *Famine in the Land: A Passionate Call for Expository Preaching* (Chicago: Moody Publishers, 2002), 42.

William Tyndale was a man who modeled the marks of bold proclamation. Born in 1494, he attended Oxford, Magdalen Hall, and Cambridge Universities. A student and adherent of the Protestant Reformation, Tyndale engaged in numerous debates with Roman Catholics. One Catholic leader chided Tyndale: "We are better to be without God's laws than the Pope." Never content to overlook heresy, Tyndale courageously replied, "I defy the Pope and all his laws. If God spare my life ere many years, I will cause the boy that drives the plow to know more of the scriptures than you."

Tyndale was a confident and bold. He was a fearless theologian and scholar who translated the Bible into an early form of Modern English, likely with the help of Martin Luther in Wittenberg. He was unjustly tried for heresy and treason in a kangaroo court and ultimately convicted. He was sent to be strangled and burnt at the stake in the prison yard on October 6, 1536. His final words were, "Lord, open the king of England's eyes." This man was anything but spineless!

Or consider the example of Thomas Cranmer (1489-1556). Cranmer served as the first Protestant Archbishop of Canterbury and helped fan the fires of Reformation in Great Britain by ensuring that the people of God could understand the Word of God.

Like Tyndale, Cranmer was committed to proclaiming the truth no matter what the cost. But his courage was tempered by grace and humility. It was said of Cranmer, "To do him any wrong was to beget a kindness from him." But kindness could not prevent his enemies from dragging him to the pyre where he would die a martyr's death. His final words before his execution bear witness to his love for his steadfast commitment to proclaim the truth:

> ... *I believe in God the Father Almighty, maker of heaven and earth, and every article of the catholic faith, every word and sentence taught by our Savior Christ, his Apostles and Prophets, in the Old and New Testaments ... And*

forasmuch as my hand offered in writing contrary to my heart, therefore my hand shall be punished; for if I may come to the fire it shall be first burned. And as for the Pope, I refuse him as Christ's enemy and Anti-christ, with all his false doctrine.[52]

Unfortunately, not everyone has the same kind of courage. Paul reveals that there are two different kinds of preachers. Some preach Christ "from envy and rivalry" (Phil. 1:15). Paul explains that this man proclaims Christ out of selfish ambition. Such a man is not sincere and proves to be unfaithful in the final analysis (v. 17). Such a man is spineless.

But some preach Christ from "good will." Paul says the motivation of this man is love (v. 16). This man understands that the apostle was providentially placed in prison for the *defense* of the gospel.

The Gospel Progressed as it was Faithfully Proclaimed

Paul's passion to proclaim the gospel is evident throughout his ministry from start to finish. He writes, " ... Only that in every way, whether in pretense or in truth, Christ is proclaimed, and in that I rejoice." (Phil. 1:18). The gospel reveals the glad tidings of the kingdom of God. The gospel is the good news. It is the proclamation of the grace of God, which is manifest and pledged in Christ.

Jesus was born of the Virgin Mary. He lived a perfect life and was tempted in every way as we are, yet without sin (Heb. 4:15). He perfectly kept the law of God. Jesus died for our sins in accordance with the Scriptures; he was buried and raised on the third day in accordance with the Scriptures (1 Cor. 15:3). Jesus was glorified and seated at the right hand of the Father. He bore the wrath of God on the cross for everyone who would ever believe (Rom. 3:25). He redeemed us from the curse of the law by becoming a curse for us (Gal. 3:13). Jesus became our

---

[52] Thomas Cranmer, cited in David Otis Fuller, *Valiant for the Truth* (New York: McGraw-Hill Book Company, Inc. 1961), 162.

substitute on the cross (2 Cor. 5:21). He reconciled us to God by making peace by the blood of his cross (Col. 1:20). He made us right with God so that we might have peace with God (Rom. 5:1). And Jesus forgives sinners and enables us to stand blameless in the presence of a holy God.

In the first century, the gospel progressed because of ferocious persecution, fearless proclamation, and faithful preaching. It was the gospel of Jesus Christ that motivated the apostle Paul. Proclaiming Christ was the driving passion of his life: "But I do not account my life of any value nor as precious to myself, if only I may finish my course and the ministry that I received from the Lord Jesus, to testify to the gospel of the grace of God" (Acts 20:24).

I had the pleasure of visiting a small church in a former communist country several years ago. The pastor was so proud of the humble little structure which was smaller than most elementary school classrooms in America. I noticed a small sign above the pulpit, written in a language that was unfamiliar to me. I asked the pastor, "What does that sign say?" He responded with a beaming smile and said through our translator: "We preach Christ crucified!" It is a moment I'll never forget.

What would it look like if each one of us committed ourselves to fearlessly and faithfully proclaiming the gospel of Jesus Christ? What would it look like if we committed ourselves to fearlessly and faithfully proclaiming the gospel in the sphere where God has placed us?

The gospel progressed because of ferocious persecution, fearless proclamation, and faithful preaching. Will you make it a goal to fearlessly and faithfully proclaim the gospel of Jesus Christ, despite the persecution that threatens you? Then and only then will we stand among the courageous. We refuse to be spineless!

6

A SECURE DWELLING PLACE

...

"Even though I walk through the valley of the shadow of death, I will fear no evil, for you are with me; your rod and your staff, they comfort me."

Psalm 23:4

J.C. Ryle stood in awe of God's precious promises:

God is continually holding out inducements to man to listen to him, obey him, and serve him, and undertaking to do great things, if man will only attend and believe ... He who has mercifully caused all Holy Scripture to be written for our learning has shown his perfect knowledge of human nature, by spreading over the Book a perfect wealth of promises, suitable to every kind of experience and every condition of life.

Concerning the variety and riches of Scripture promises, far more might be said than it is possible to say in a short paper like this. Their name is legion. The subject is almost inexhaustible. There is a hardly a step in a man's life, from childhood to old age, hardly any position in which man can be placed, for which the Bible has not held out encouragement to everyone who desires to do right in the sight of God. There are 'shalls' and 'wills' in God's treasury for every condition. About God's infinite mercy and compassion - about his readiness to receive all who repent and believe - about his willingness to forgive, pardon, and absolve the chief of sinners – about his power to change hearts and alter our corrupt nature – about the encouragements to pray, and hear the gospel, and draw near to the throne of grace – about strength for duty, comfort in trouble guidance in perplexity, help in sickness, consolation in death, support under bereavement, happiness beyond the grave, reward in glory – about all these things there is an abundant supply of promises in the Word.[53]

The promises of God are a comfort in the midst of difficultly and help bolster our resolve in days of suffering. One such promise occurs in Psalm 23:4.

Even though I walk through the valley of the shadow of death, I will fear no evil, for you are with me; your rod and your staff, they comfort me.

This promise will help strengthen us and grant courage in our daily lives.

A CRITICAL PROMISE

He Emboldens Us with His Presence

The psalmist assumes something in Psalm 23:4. He assumes that we will walk through the valley of the shadow of death. This valley could include suffering. It could involve pain. It could mean persecution. Whatever the case, we find the psalmist in dire straits. When Adam and Eve disobeyed God, they fell under the curse (Gen. 2:17; 3:16-19). So walking in the valley of the shadow of death comes as no surprise. It comes as a consequence of sin. The author of Psalm 23 is in touch with reality. He does not try to hide his adversity. Like the apostle Paul (2 Cor. 11:23-28), David faces his suffering directly.

The response of the psalmist is a great help and encouragement for Christians who seek to jettison the path of spinelessness. David says, "I will fear no evil" (v. 4). One of the repeated themes of Scripture is *fear not*. Over and over again, we are re-

---

[53] J.C. Ryle, *Holiness: Its Nature, Hindrances, Difficulties, and Roots*, 361-363.

minded and admonished to *fear not*. A small sampling of passages demonstrates the importance of Christian courage:

> *And the LORD appeared to him the same night and said, "I am the God of Abraham your father. Fear not, for I am with you and will bless you and multiply your offspring for my servant Abraham's sake (Gen. 26:24).*

> *Though an army encamp against me, my heart shall not fear; though war arise against me, yet I will be confident (Ps. 27:3).*

> *The LORD is on my side; I will not fear. What can man do to me? (Ps. 118:6).*

> *... Fear not, for I am with you; be not dismayed, for I am your God; I will strengthen you, I will help you, I will uphold you with my righteous right hand (Isa. 41:10).*

> *For I, the LORD your God, hold your right hand; it is I who say to you, 'Fear not, I am the one who helps you' (Isa. 41:13).*

> *Fear not, you worm Jacob, you men of Israel! I am the one who helps you, declares the LORD; your Redeemer is the Holy One of Israel (Isa. 41:14).*

> *They know not, nor do they discern, for he has shut their eyes, so that they cannot see, and their hearts, so that they cannot understand (Isa. 44:18).*

> *Fear not, O land; be glad and rejoice, for the LORD has done great things! (Joel 2:21).*

> *There is no fear in love, but perfect love casts out fear. For fear has to do with punishment, and whoever fears has not been perfected in love (1 John 4:18).*

Since David has committed himself to this posture of fearlessness, he lives in security: "I will fear no evil, for you are with me; your rod and your staff, they comfort me" (v. 4). In other words, God *comforted* and *emboldened* David with his presence. John Frame explains the importance of covenant presence, namely - "that God commits himself to us, to be our God and to make us his people. He delivers us by his grace and rules us by his law, and he rules not only from above, but also with us and within us."[54] David maintains the shepherding metaphor and speaks of God's rod and staff and the comfort they bring him (Isa. 40:11).

Think for a moment about how God comforts and emboldens you with his covenant presence. I don't know what the "valley of the shadow of death" looks like for you right now. I understand it can be frightening. Maybe you are enduring a season of persecution. You may be in a struggling marriage. Your job is about to break you. You received a devastating diagnosis from your physician. Whatever the case, please understand that the Shepherd is with you in the valley. I urge you to stand with David and acknowledge the valley. But I also urge you to stand with David and say, "I will fear no evil." The Shepherd promises to embolden you with his covenant presence. He will provide a secure dwelling place. The Shepherd will enable you to flee from spinelessness.

---

[54] John M. Frame, *The Doctrine of God* (Phillipsburg: Presbyterian & Reformed, 2002), 96.

A STALWART TRUST IN THE SOVEREIGNTY OF GOD

---... ---

*"Wrong will be right when Aslan comes in sight, At the
sound of his roar, sorrows will be no more, when he bears
his teeth, winter meets its death, and when he shakes his
mane, we shall have spring again."*[55]

C.S. Lewis

T he psalmist models what it means to turn to the Lord
in Psalm 121:1-8.

> *I lift up my eyes to the hills. From where does my help
> come? My help comes from the LORD, who made heav-
> en and earth. He will not let your foot be moved; he who
> keeps you will not slumber. Behold, he who keeps Israel
> will neither slumber nor sleep. The LORD is your keep-
> er; the LORD is your shade on your right hand. The sun
> shall not strike you by day, nor the moon by night. The
> LORD will keep you from all evil; he will keep your life.
> The LORD will keep your going out and your coming in
> from this time forth and forevermore.*

TURN TO THE LORD

In Old Testament, Jewish people would make their way to Jerusalem for the annual feasts. Since there were no conventional

---

[55] C.S. Lewis, *The Lion, the Witch and the Wardrobe* (1950; New York: Harper-
Collins, 2000), 79.

roads in those days, it's easy to see how this psalm would have provided encouragement for the weary traveler. Imagine making your way to Jerusalem. Your bones ache. Your throat is parched. Fear is your constant companion. And suddenly you see the hills of Judah: "I lift up my eyes to the hills. From where does my help come? My help comes from the Lord, who made heaven and earth" (Ps. 121:1–2).

C.H. Spurgeon helps us understand the mindset of the Jewish traveler: "The purposes of God; the divine attributes; the immutable promises; the covenant, ordered in all things and sure; the providence, predestination, and proved the faithfulness of the Lord - these are the hills to which we must lift up our eyes, and from these our help must come."[56] We are to direct our attention to a sovereign God who has our best interests in mind.

Psalm 121 teaches us that turning to the Lord involves two important components. First, it involves *a heart that is riveted on God* (v. 1). This is a proactive look; a look that is intentional. Riveting our hearts on God does not happen by accident. It is deliberate and purposeful. It is an act of the will. Indeed, this is a look that is captivated by our glorious God who finds great delight in working for us. The prophet Isaiah adds, "From of old no one has heard or perceived by the ear, no eye has seen a God besides you, who acts for those who wait for him" (Isa. 64:4). The safest place for us, then, is to cast our gaze upon the living God.

This is a disciplined look, one that is governed by biblical conviction and informed by truth. Paul writes, "Have nothing to do with irreverent, silly myths. Rather train yourself for godliness (1 Tim. 4:7). *Gumnádzō*, the Greek term for *train* is also translated as "discipline" (NAS) and "exercise" (KJV). Paul employs this athletic metaphor for obvious reasons, calling believers to a life of disciplined pursuit, much like a sprinter who trains to win the prize. In a similar fashion, we are called to discipline ourselves for the purpose of godliness.

---

[56] Charles Haddon Spurgeon, *The Treasury of David - Volume 3* (Peabody: Hendrickson), 14.

This is an informed look. A heart that is riveted on God, banks on his character. Therefore, an informed look is one that consistently turns to the Scripture in order to gain a clear portrait of God. King David understood the importance of the informed look, as we find him clinging to the biblical portrait of God: "Yours O LORD, is the greatness and the power and the glory and the victory and the majesty, for all that is in the heavens and in the earth is yours. Yours is the kingdom, O LORD, and you are exalted as head above all" (1 Chron. 29:11). He understood that God is worthy of our trust, adoration, reverence, and worship.

This is a look that acknowledges need; one that gazes upon the majesty of God and finds help in his all-sufficient hands. Whenever we acknowledge our need, as Christ-followers we gravitate to the One who has the ability to meet our needs. We turn to our great God whom Isaiah describes as a sheep herder who cares for his people: "He will tend his flock like a shepherd; he will gather the lambs in his arms; he will carry them in his bosom, and gently lead those that are with young" (Isa. 40:11).

And this is a look of faith. Whenever we direct our gaze to God, we demonstrate faith. This is the kind of faith that is riveted on God. This is the kind of faith that pleases God. "And without faith it is impossible to please him for whoever would draw near to God must believe that he exists and that he rewards those who seek him" (Heb. 11:6). Turning to the Lord, then, involves a heart that is riveted on God.

Second, it involves *a heart that runs to God* (v. 2). A heart that runs to God is quick to seek his face:

> *But from there you will seek the LORD your God and you will find him, if you search after him with all your heart and with all your soul (Deut. 4:29).*

> *If my people who are called by my name humble themselves, and pray and seek my face and turn from their wicked ways, then I will hear from heaven and will forgive their sin and heal their land (2 Chron. 7:14).*

We see this quality in the psalmist as he cries out, "My help comes from the LORD, who made heaven and earth" (Ps. 121:2).

A heart that runs to God is humble. Humility is "honestly assessing ourselves in light of God's holiness and our sinfulness."[57] The Old Testament word for humility means "to be gentle; i.e. pertaining to being unpretentious and straightforward, suggesting a lack of arrogance, hubris, or pride."[58] Several passages in the Old Testament help clarify the meaning of this important concept:

> *Toward the scorners he is scornful, but to the humble he gives favor (Prov. 3:34).*

> *Rejoice greatly, O daughter of Zion! Shout aloud, O daughter of Jerusalem! Behold, your king is coming to you; righteous and having salvation is he, humble and mounted on a donkey, on a colt, the foal of a donkey (Zech. 9:9).*

> *You save a humble people, but your eyes are on the haughty to bring them down (2 Sam. 22:28).*

A heart that runs to God receives mercy. The psalmist cries out, "Hear the voice of my pleas for mercy, when I cry to you for help, when I left up my hands toward your most holy sanctuary" (Ps. 28:2).

And a heart that runs to God is delivered and receives salvation: "Help us, O God of our salvation, for the glory of your name; deliver us, and atone for our sins, for your name's sake" (Ps. 79:9).

So Psalm 121:1-2 urges us to turn to the LORD. But why does it make good sense to turn to the LORD? Notice at least three reasons for doing so:

First, the Scriptures demand that we turn to the LORD.

But from there you will seek the Lord your God and you

---

[57] C.J. Mahaney, Humility: True Greatness (Wheaton: Crossway Books, 2005), 22.

[58] Swanson, J. (1997). Dictionary of Biblical Languages with Semantic Domains: Hebrew (Old Testament). Oak Harbor: Logos Research Systems, Inc.

*will find him, if you search after him with all your heart
and with all your soul (Deut. 4:29).*

*... if my people who are called by my name humble them-
selves, and pray and seek my face and turn from their
wicked ways, then I will hear from heaven and will forgive their sin and heal their land (2 Chron. 7:14).*

Second, we turn to the LORD because he is the maker of
heaven and earth.

*For thus says the Lord, who created the heavens (he is
God!), who formed the earth and made it (he established
it; he did not create it empty, he formed it to be inhabited!):
'I am the Lord, and there is no other' (Isa. 45:18).*

*Our help is in the name of the Lord, who made heaven
and earth (Ps. 124:8).*

*May the Lord bless you from Zion, he who made heaven
and earth! (Ps. 134:3).*

Here is a challenge to every evolutionist: When you are at
the end of your rope, you call out to dark, empty space. You have
nothing. You have no hope! But followers of Christ have a deep
and abiding hope as they turn to God, the maker of heaven and
earth.

There is a third reason we are called upon to turn to the
LORD and it involves a blessing. There is a blessing for everyone who turn to the LORD (Ps. 115:11-16). Not everyone responds like the psalmist in Psalm 121. Often times, when people
need help, they turn to cheap substitutes. When people are at
the end of their rope, they turn to pills. They turn to the bottle.
They turn to psychology or philosophy. They turn to self-help
books. They rely on Oprah and Dr. Phil. They turn to Deepak
Chopra, Wayne Dyer, or Anthony Robbins. They surf the inter-
net. They invade the library, searching high and low for answers.
Yet all along, they neglect the One who made the heavens and
the earth. They neglect their only source of hope - the living
God. Oprah and Dr. Phil did not make the heaven and earth.
The self-help gurus did not create the cosmos.

We have seen what turning to the LORD involves. Notice, however, the primary characteristic of the person who turns away from the LORD. Such a turning from God involves the mother of all sins, namely, the sin of pride.

Proud people are a law unto themselves, which is the very essence of autonomy. Proud people make the rules. They call the shots. Proud people create so-called "autonomous zones," like we witnessed recently in Seattle. No one, not even God tells the proud person what to do. Proud people place confidence in their abilities. Foolishly, they trust themselves. It's no wonder that the self-help publishing industry is exploding. They cater to proud people. Proud people don't have time for the Bible. Proud people do not need divine revelation. They don't have time for God. They are autonomous.

An example of a man who turned away from God is Nebuchadnezzar. In Daniel 4, we find him strutting on the roof of the royal palace of Babylon: "Is not this great Babylon, which I have built by my mighty power as a royal residence and for the glory of my majesty?" (v. 30). Nebuchadnezzar is confronted by God:

> *While the words were still in the king's mouth, there fell a voice from heaven, 'O King Nebuchadnezzar, to you it is spoken: The kingdom has departed from you, and you shall be driven from among men, and your dwelling shall be with the beasts of the field. And you shall be made to eat grass like an ox, and seven periods of time shall pass over you, until you know that the Most High rules the kingdom of men and gives it to whom he will.' Immediately the word was fulfilled against Nebuchadnezzar. He was driven from among men and ate grass like an ox, and his body was wet with the dew of heaven till his hair grew as long as eagles' feathers, and his nails were like birds' claws (Dan. 4:31–33).*

The consequences of pride is a sobering reality. The Scripture teaches that pride comes before a fall (Prov. 16:18). Pride is numbered among the sins that God hates (Prov. 8:13). Therefore, the proud cannot stand in God's presence. Isaiah 2:17 says,

"And the haughtiness of man shall be humbled, and the lofty pride of men shall be brought low, and the LORD alone will be exalted in that day." And in the end, we learn that the proud person is actually opposed by God (Jas. 4:6).

So where should we go when we're at the end of our rope? To be sure, resisting God and refusing his leadership and lordship in our lives is not the path we want to pursue. We choose to follow the lead of the Psalmist by *turning to the Lord*. In so doing, our hearts will be riveted on God. Our hearts will joyfully run to God.

But Scripture not only calls us to turn to the Lord. We are called to trust in the Lord as well.

TRUST IN THE LORD

I want you to see something very important. I want you to see that God not only made the heaven and the earth (Ps. 121:2). He also sustains it and controls it. Indeed, God governs all things for his glory (Col. 1:16-17; Heb. 1:3).

The *Westminster Confession of Faith* summarizes the important biblical doctrine of providence:

> God, the great Creator of all things, doth uphold, direct, dispose, and govern all creatures, actions, and things, from the greatest even to the least, by his most holy wise and holy providence, according to his infallible fore-knowledge, and the free and immutable counsel of his own will, to the praise of the glory of his wisdom, power, justice, goodness, and mercy.[59]

The confession clearly teaches that:

- God created all things and sustains all things (Col. 1:16-17; Heb. 1:3).

- God exercises complete control over all things. Therefore, the notion of "fate" or "chance" is a pagan idea (Prov. 21:1).

---

[59] G.I. Williamson, Ed. *The Westminster Confession of Faith* (Philipsburg: Presbyterian and Reformed, 1964), 60

- God's control over all things extends to the actions of creatures and all the events in the natural world (Prov. 19:21; Job 37:9-13).
- The ultimate end culminates to the praise of God's glory (Eph. 1:11).

Divine Protection

The verb *keep* occurs at least six times in this passage. I think there is a specific reason that the psalmist chose this word. The term means "to watch over, guard, or preserve; to be secure or protect."

God providentially protects his people (v. 3). "God, who watches over his own, will not slumber or sleep, that is he will not be indifferent to or disregard them. The Lord will be alert in protecting his own."[60]

God providentially protects Israel (v. 4). Notice that the One who promises to protect his people never sleeps and never slumbers. He never takes a break. He never needs someone else to take his shift (Ps. 90:2).

God providentially provides for the needs of his people (vv. 5-6). Notice the comprehensive nature of this divine help - "the sun shall not strike you by day, nor the moon by night."

God providentially protects his people from evil. "The Lord will keep you from all evil; he will keep your life" (Ps. 121:7). What a wonderful summary that includes a mighty promise: God providentially protects his people and provides for his people.

Application

Turning to the LORD and trusting in the LORD are the marks of a God-centered faith, a faith that banks on the promises of God. So let me leave you with several practical points of application.

---

[60] Ross, A.P (1985). *Psalms*. (J.F. Walvoord & R.B. Zuck, Eds.) T*he Bible Knowledge Commentary: An Exposition of the Scriptures* (Vol. 1, 883). Wheaton, IL: Victor Books.

1. *Nothing, absolutely nothing can touch our lives without God's permission* (Rom. 8:35-39).

2. *God's providential control over all things extinguishes our fear.* "When I am afraid, I put my trust in you. In God, whose word I praise, in God I trust; I shall not be afraid ..." (Ps. 56:3-4). God's providence reminds us that when faith reigns, fear is powerless. When faith reigns, fear is erased.

3. *God's providential control over all things builds our faith.* C.H. Spurgeon adds:

> *I believe that every particle of dust that dances in the sunbeam does not move an atom more or less than God wishes—that every particle of spray that dashes against the steamboat has its orbit as well as the sun in the heavens - that the chaff from the hand of the winnower is steered as the stars in the courses. The creeping of an aphid over the rosebud is as much fixed as the march of the devastating pestilence—the fall of sere leaves from a poplar is as fully ordained as the tumbling of an avalanche. He that believes in a God must believe this truth. There is no standing-point between this and atheism. There is no halfway between an almighty God that worth all things by the sovereign control of his will and no God at all. A God that cannot do as he pleases—a God whose will is frustrated, is not a God, and cannot be a God. I could not believe in such a God as that.*[61]

4. *When we believe the promises of God, he is greatly glorified.*

MY HOPE IS FOUND IN NOTHING LESS

When you are at the end of your rope, turn to the LORD and trust in the LORD. You may be at the end of your rope with a friend

---

[61] C.H. Spurgeon, *Spurgeon Sermons - Volume 2, God's Providence* (Grand Rapids: Baker Books, 1883), 201.

or loved one. Turn to the LORD and trust the LORD. You may be at the end of your rope in your marriage. Turn to the LORD and trust the LORD. Others of you are at the end of your rope as you face a temptation of some kind. You are close to giving in. You must turn to the LORD and trust the LORD.

When you are at the end of your rope, turn to the LORD and trust in the LORD. In doing so, you will be running to the cross. You will be clinging to the cross. You will be trusting in the merits of Christ on the cross!

I want to encourage you to model after the prayer of the psalmist. When you lift your eyes unto the hills, won't you cry out, "From where does my help come? My help comes from the LORD, who made heaven and earth!" When you are at the end of your rope, turn to the LORD and trust in the LORD who is sovereign in creation and sovereign over creation. A stalwart trust in God will lead you on path away from spinelessness.

⇒ PART 3 ⇐

THE RALLY CRY OF COURAGE AND CONVICTION
———— ••• ————

*"Heavenly Father, I give thee most hearty thanks that
thou hast called me to a profession of thee even unto
death. I beseech thee, Lord God, have mercy on this realm
of England, and deliver the same from all her enemies."*

Nicholas Ridley

THIS MEANS WAR

*"Be strong, and let your heart take courage, all you who
wait for the LORD!"*

Psalm 31:24

In part one, we diagnosed the decline of courage and conviction. We witnessed some of the brave souls who stood in the gap for the sake of truth in Scripture and redemptive history.

In part two, we pled for a recovery of courage and conviction. Such an ambitious plan requires a supercharged prayer for courage, a staunch allegiance to the Word of God, a steadfast commitment to proclaim the truth, and a stalwart trust in the sovereignty of God.

We conclude our journey in part three with a rally cry for courage and conviction. Our task is to steer clear from a spineless form of Christianity that cowers before men and capitulates the truth of God's Word.

DIVINE PERSPECTIVE

In Paul's letter to the church at Ephesus, the apostle took the first century believers to the peak of the mountain and helped them see the panorama of God's blessings. He also ushers each subsequent leader to the summit of Mt. Everest and unfolds the beauty of God's grace and the rich blessings that he showers upon his people.

In the book of Ephesians, we learn that the fountainhead of all the blessings that we receive find their origin in God the Father. Each of these blessings are spiritual blessings which are linked to the Lord Jesus Christ. These blessings are totally undeserved. It is here that we learn about our inheritance, which is predestined according to the counsel of his will (Eph. 1:11).

In Ephesians chapter 2, Paul reveals that we were dead in trespasses and sins and that we were saved by grace alone through faith alone, in Christ alone. We learn that we can never be saved by works but that we were made *for* good works. That is, justifying faith always leads the people of God to bear fruit. "For we are his workmanship, created in Christ Jesus for good works, which God prepared beforehand, that we should walk in them" (Eph. 2:10).

Additionally, we learn in chapter two that Christian maturity demands rejoicing:

- We are friends with God (v. 13).
- We have peace with God (vv. 14-15).
- We have been reconciled to God (v. 16).

We are citizens of God's kingdom (Eph. 2:19). This citizenship involves a host of unique privileges and also implies some very important responsibilities. We are members of God's family:

> So then you are no longer strangers and aliens, but you are fellow citizens with the saints and members of the household of God, built on the foundation of the apostles and prophets, Christ Jesus himself being the cornerstone, in whom the whole structure, being joined together, grows into a holy temple in the Lord. In him you also are being built together into a dwelling place for God by the Spirit (Eph. 2:19–22).

In Ephesians chapter 3, we bear witness to the drama of the gospel:

- The mystery of the gospel.

- The ministry of the gospel.

- The motive of the gospel.

- The might of the gospel.

The drama of the gospel reminds us to maintain a God-centered perspective:

- When we suffer, we remind ourselves of the gospel.

- When we feel weak, we remind ourselves of the gospel.

- When we feel overwhelmed, we remind ourselves of the gospel.

- When life spins out of control, we remind ourselves of the gospel.

- When we grow discouraged, we remind ourselves of the gospel.

In Ephesians chapter 4, Paul helps us understand the importance of maintaining unity in the body of Christ (4:1-6). Additionally, we learn the importance of growing into mature disciples. Indeed, God blesses the church with spiritual leadership so she might be mature (4:7-12). And we learn the importance of dwelling together in the City of God, where we put off our old self (4:22), aim for renewal (4:23), and put on the new self (4:24). In the City of God, we are committed to the truth and committed to controlled emotions, conscientious hands, and clean lips. Ultimately, we are committed to living for God's glory!

In Ephesians chapter 5, Paul continues to focus intensely on our conduct, which is riveted on God. "Be imitators of God," the apostle says (5:1). Our responsibility is to "walk in love" (5:2). We are called to walk in purity (5:3-4). Specifically, we are called to:

- Be careful how we walk (vv. 15-16).

- Be consumed with God's will (v. 17).

- Be controlled by the Holy Spirit (vv. 18-20).

We also learn about the importance of biblical submission, which is applied across the board to wives, husbands, children, and employees. No one is exempt and no one is excluded.

In Ephesians chapter 6, Paul's letter draws to a close. It is penned for the benefit, instruction, and encouragement of God's people. After all that Paul has written about, including the rich blessings that belong to every follower of Christ; after all the gospel-centered hope that we enjoy in this life and the life to come; after all the realities of the gospel that have literally exploded into our lives, Paul *assumes something*. He assumes a struggle.

You have likely heard the gospel presented in such a way that seemed to promise that all your problems would vanish if you embraced the Christian faith. This is one of the many vacuous promises offered by the so-called prosperity gospel, which is no gospel at all. The prosperity gospel is an anti-gospel. It stands opposed to the gospel of Jesus Christ. But even those who rightly reject this pernicious movement can easily fall into a kind of thinking which seems to suggest that struggles will cease when one becomes a Christian. Nothing could be further from the truth. In some respects, you might say that when a person becomes a Christian, the struggle truly begins to take shape.

The reality is that the Christian life involves intense and ongoing struggle. There will be days of discouragement. There will be days of depression. There will be days which are filled with doubt. There will be days of darkness. And there will be days of disaster. It is in the context of this struggle that the Word of God offers a solution which enables our hands for battle. It is in the context of this struggle that the apostle Paul sets forth the *proper mindset* and the *proper methodology* on the battlefield.

It is time for followers of Jesus Christ to stand up and be counted. It is time to "wage the good warfare, holding faith and a good conscience" (1 Tim. 1:18-19). "Now is the time," says John MacArthur, "for the strongest men to preach the strongest message in the context of the strongest ministry." It is time for

Christians in this generation to open their eyes to reality. It is time to wake up and view things with fresh perspective that is in alignment with the Word of God!

DIVINE COURAGE

One of the greatest needs of our generation is divine courage. The church in the twenty-first century, as we have seen, can accurately be described as *spineless*. We are weak-kneed and fearful. We are passive. Such is the state of the contemporary church. We have lost our nerve. We lack theological depth. We lack theological backbone. We are spineless!

The twenty-first century church also lacks conviction. For the most part, we do not possess the fiery faith of the Puritans. We do not possess the bold resolve of the Reformers. Indeed, we are spineless!

Ephesians 6:10 entreats believers, "Finally, be strong in the Lord and in the strength of his might." Notice three things about this crucial verse:

First, it is a *command*. The Greek word translated, *strong* means "to be rendered capable or able for a task." In this case, Paul is referring to divine capability or spiritual strength on the battlefield. That is, we are called to be strong and courageous in the Christian life. The call to courage is found throughout Scripture:

> *Only be strong and very courageous, being careful to do according to all the law that Moses my servant commanded you. Do not turn from it to the right hand or to the left, that you may have good success wherever you go (Josh. 1:7).*

> *Be of good courage, and let us be courageous for our people, and for the cities of our God, and may the LORD do what seems good to him (2 Sam. 10:12).*

> *Wait for the LORD; be strong, and let your heart take courage; wait for the LORD! (Ps. 27:14).*

> *Be strong, and let your heart take courage, all you who wait for the LORD! (Ps. 31:24).*

So we are always of good courage. We know that while we are at home in the body we are away from the Lord ... (2 Cor. 5:6).

Throughout the Old Testament, God commands Israel to *fear not:*

You shall not fear them, for it is the LORD your God who fights for you (Deut. 3:22).

Though an army encamp against me, my heart shall not fear; though war arise against me, yet I will be confident (Ps. 27:3).

You will not fear the terror of the night, nor the arrow that flies by day (Ps. 91:5).

When I am afraid, I put my trust in you. In God, whose word I praise, in God I trust; I shall not be afraid. What can flesh do to me? (Ps. 56:3–4).

The LORD is on my side; I will not fear. What can man do to me? (Ps. 118:6).

Second, Ephesians 6:10 is *centered* on the Lord Jesus Christ. The command to "be strong" is a plea for spiritual courage, which is grounded in the person and work of Jesus. Apart from Christ, we are weak and frail. Without him, we are hopeless. Without him, we can do nothing (John 15:5).

The apostle Paul's life and theology were centered on Jesus Christ. He wrote to the believers in Philippi, "I can do all things through him who strengthens me" (Phil. 4:13). He encouraged his young protégé, Timothy to "be strengthened by the grace that is in Christ Jesus" (2 Tim. 2:1). And he confessed, "But the Lord stood by me and strengthened me, so that through me the message might be fully proclaimed and all the Gentiles might hear it. So I was rescued from the lion's mouth" (2 Tim. 4:17).

Observe how Paul piles on a few terms in Ephesians 6:10. He calls us to be **strong** in the Lord in the **strength** of his **might**. The Greek word translated *strength* means "to direct, determine or govern." And the Greek word translated *might* means, "God's ability to get the job done." Scripture speaks in candid terms about the mighty power of the Lord:

> *Then he said to me, 'This is the word of the LORD to Zerubbabel: Not by might, nor by power, but by my Spirit, says the LORD of hosts' (Zech. 4:6).*

> *I have been crucified with Christ. It is no longer I who live, but Christ who lives in me. And the life I now live in the flesh I live by faith in the Son of God, who loved me and gave himself for me (Gal. 2:20).*

The command to *be strong in the Lord in the strength of his might* means that we trust Jesus; we trust his strength; we trust in his might. Again, God's Word testifies to the power of people who trust in the Lord:

> *Israel saw the great power that the LORD used against the Egyptians, so the people feared the LORD, and they believed in the LORD and in his servant Moses (Exod. 14:31).*

> *Your right hand, O LORD, glorious in power, your right hand, O LORD, shatters the enemy (Exod. 15:6).*

> *Yours, O LORD, is the greatness and the power and the glory and the victory and the majesty, for all that is in the heavens and in the earth is yours. Yours is the kingdom, O LORD, and you are exalted as head above all. Both riches and honor come from you, and you rule over all. In your hand are power and might, and in your hand it is to make great and to give strength to all (1 Chron. 29:12).*

Third, Ephesians 6:10 is *counterintuitive*. Conventional wisdom instructs us to go it alone.

- People find strength in their own wisdom.
- People find strength in their own abilities.
- People find strength in their own ingenuity.
- People find strength in their own resources.
- People find strength in their own flesh.

Yet, the Word of God tells us to stop trusting ourselves. The Word of God tells us that our so-called "righteousness" is like filthy rags in the sight of God (Isa. 64:6). So Scripture commands, "Be strong in the Lord and in the strength of his might." Indeed, it is counterintuitive.

Do you find daily strength in the Lord or do you jettison this command and seek to live in the strength of your flimsy flesh? Here is a crucial question: When you consider the God who parted the Red Sea, rescued Israel from Pharaoh, delivered the men from the fiery furnace, and raised Jesus from the grave - why would anyone trust anyone less that the living God? Proverbs 14:12 says, "There is a way that seems right to a man, but its end is the way to death."

DIVINE ENABLEMENT

The marching orders are clearly set forth in Ephesians 6:1-12. Paul writes, "Put on the whole armor of God, that you may be able to stand against the schemes of the devil. For we do not wrestle against flesh and blood, but against the rulers, against the authorities, against the cosmic powers over this present darkness, against the spiritual forces of evil in the heavenly places" (Eph. 6:11–12).

First, it is a *command*. Paul urges believers to *put on* the whole armor of God. The armor is described in verses 14-17 and includes the belt of truth, the breastplate of righteousness, the shoes of the gospel of peace, the shield of faith, the helmet of salvation, and the sword of the Spirit. The command to *put on* the whole armor of God is an *act of the will*. Putting on the whole armor of God is also *an act of faith*.

Second, it is *comprehensive*. Paul calls believers to put on the whole armor of God. Indeed, neglecting any piece of armor is not only an act of disobedience; it also leads to spiritually disastrous results. To illustrate, a football player could wear his knee pads, girdle, and shoulder pads. But if a player refuses to wear his helmet, he will eventually end up with a head injury. Likewise, if we neglect the helmet of salvation in the Christian life, we are asking for trouble.

Third, it is *constructive*. Putting on the armor of God equips us for a very important task. The armor enables us to stand against the schemes of the devil. The devil's schemes (*methodeia*) are his deceptive tactics designed to lure us away from God, the Word of God, and the people of God. The Bible says that the devil disguises himself as an angel of light (2 Cor. 11:14). Indeed, he is a murder. He is the father of lies (John 8:44). He is a thief who comes to steal, kill, and destroy (John 10:10). And he is a great deceiver (Rev. 12:9).

The devil has been deceiving from the beginning (Gen. 3:1-5). The devil distorts the truth. He distracts the people of God. "The best thing, where it is possible," says Lewis's Screwtape, "is to keep the patient (the follower of Christ) from the serious intention of praying altogether."[62]

Additionally, the devil works hard to instill doubt in people. He seeks to discourage people. For example, Martin Luther battled depression most of his adult life. In 1527, he wrote, "For more than a week I was close to the gates of death and hell."[63] The devil seeks to disarm people. He loves it when believers neglect the command to put on the whole armor of God. Never let us forget - the arch enemy of our souls is on a mission to destroy the people of God. So the command to put on the whole armor of God is constructive. It enables us to stand against the schemes of the devil.

Fourth, it is *calculated*. Paul describes the battlefield in clear and unambiguous terms: "For we do not wrestle against flesh and blood, but against rulers, against the authorities, against the cosmic powers over this present darkness, against the spiritual forces of evil in the heavenly places" (Eph. 6:12). *Wrestle (pálei)* is

---

[62] C.S. Lewis, *The Screwtape Letters* (New York: MacMillan Publishing Company, 1961), 19-20.

[63] Martin Luther, cited in Roland Bainton, *Here I Stand* (New York: New American Library, n.d), 282.

"the act of engaging in close hand-to-hand combat." What Paul says here is critically important. He does not assume a struggle as he did in verse 10. Rather, he says it overtly: We are in a serious struggle. We are in a battle of epic proportions. Yet, that struggle is not against flesh and blood. That is, our struggle is not with other people. Our struggle is in the spiritual arena. Our struggle is against:

> *Rulers (àrchei)* - *"Any supernatural being (besides God) acting in a ruling or commanding capacity."*
>
> *Authorities (éxousia)* - *"A person who exercises administrative control over others."*
>
> *Cosmic powers (kosmokrátor)* - *"Supernatural powers; the godless worldly system."*
>
> *Spiritual forces of evil (poneiria) in the heavenly places.*

Our struggle is with the forces of evil that oppose God, the Word of God, and the gospel of Jesus Christ. This struggle is supernatural. We fight in vain in our own strength.

In verse 13, Paul repeats the command in a slightly different way: "Take up the whole armor of God. This too, is a *command*. This is also *comprehensive* as Paul urges Christ-followers to take up the whole armor of God. And this is *constructive*. Paul has a specific aim for the Ephesian believers. And he has a specific aim for each one of us.

The primary reason we are called to take up the whole armor of God is so that we may be able to withstand the evil one. When we take up the whole armor of God, we are granted supernatural power to do two things:

Withstand: God enables us to "withstand in the evil day" (Eph. 6:13). The term translated withstand means "to express opposition to something; to resist or oppose something." In this case, God gives us a supernatural ability to withstand the attacks of the enemy.

Stand firm: God also enables us to stand firm. Mark Vroegop makes this sober plea: "In the midst of the darkest moments of your life, I hope you'll have the courage and conviction to say, 'But I call to mind what God is like. I'm going to rehearse what I know to be true. I'm going to recite what I know I believe. I'm going to dare to hope.'[64] We are granted courage in the face of adversity. God is faithful to instill conviction in the midst of suffering. We are granted supernatural ability to withstand the forces of darkness and stand firm.

Every person is in a cosmic struggle. It is an epic battle that is spiritual in nature. You may be struggling with doubt. Does God exist? Does he care about me? Did he send his Son to die for me? Is the Word of God true? You may be depressed or discouraged. Perhaps you are facing some kind of inner turmoil that is eating you up inside. You may be battling guilt for something that took place years ago. You may be on the slippery slope of temptation. Maybe you're ready to chuck your wedding vows. You may even be toying with abandoning your long-held beliefs in God and his Word. You may be battling some kind of sexual sin that will ruin your reputation. You may be on the brink of rebellion. You may have suicidal thoughts. You may feel like giving up the race.

Brother or sister, it's time to wake up and view things with fresh perspective. It's time to see things through a lens that magnifies the great God of the universe! To be sure, there is a battle. The battle is intense. The battle is deeply spiritual. You must remember this, however - *the battle has already been won!*

> *And you, who were dead in your trespasses and the uncir-*
> *cumcision of your flesh, God made alive together with*

---

[64] Mark Vroegop, *Dark Clouds, Deep Mercy: Discovering the Grace of Lament* (Wheaton: Crossway, 2019), 111.

him, having forgiven us all our trespasses, by canceling the record of debt that stood against us with its legal demands. This he set aside, nailing it to the cross. He disarmed the rulers and authorities and put them to open shame, by triumphing over them in him (Col. 2:13–15).

God is calling you to be bold. He is calling you to be brave. *He requires divine courage and divine enablement in order to be effective on the battlefield.* Anything less is spineless.

9

SETTING THE "SPIRITUAL BAR"

—— ··· ——

*"But one certain indicator that God has called a man is
that he stands firm and perseveres in ministry after he has
been thoroughly buffeted by a hurricane of affliction."*[65]

Jeff Robinson

MARCHING ORDERS

"Pastor, we need to talk." The request was not new or novel by
any stretch of the imagination. Giving spiritual counsel is a part
of the landscape of pastoral ministry. But this request was different. This request had a sense of urgency attached to it. I knew it
was serious. So I prayed and prepared for the worst.

My friend and I arranged for a time to meet and share a
meal. After we placed our orders, I learned that my suspicions
were correct. This brother was in trouble - deep trouble. He pro-
ceeded to share a prolonged battle with pornography. After this
man lamented and confessed his sin, I looked him dead in the
eye and challenged him. It is a challenge that he and I still refer
to from time to time. Lifting both of my hands high into the air,
I said, "You need to commit right here and right now to never
look at pornography again. Ever!"

---

[65] Cited in Collin Hansen and Jeff Robinson, Eds. *12 Faithful Men: Portraits of
Courageous Endurance in Pastoral Ministry* (Grand Rapids: Baker Books, 2018), 29.

When I challenged my friend that day, I set the "spiritual bar." My friend has since told me that the challenge appeared crazy. It seemed impossible given his previous battle with pornography. But he accepted the challenge, confessed his sin to his wife, and we began to craft a battle plan for purity.

Several years later, after a season of pronounced study, prayer, and accountability, this man is exercising his spiritual gifts in his local church, leading his family, and continues to walk by God's grace in purity. He is an example to other men of what it means to surrender to the Spirit of God and live by faith for God's glory.

Spineless men let culture dictate their values and worldviews. Spineless men cave in when the chips are down. Spineless men don't know the first thing about courage or conviction. Courageous men are different, however. Courageous men are undergirded by unwavering biblical convictions. These men are bold and brave. They know what they believe. They are not only prepared to defend the truth. They are eager to live the truth.

Men of courage and conviction set a high "spiritual bar." "Men," says Ron Schaeffer, set the spiritual thermometer of a home or church."[66] The fruitfulness of our homes and churches, then, is dependent on men who exert strong, humble, and God-centered leadership. Weak men spawn weak homes and weak churches. Men of courage and conviction lead homes and churches that bear spiritual fruit to the glory of God.

The very notion of masculinity is rooted in Scripture and is covenantal in scope. God calls us to be "leaders and servants in the ultimate cause of displaying God's glory and bearing the fruit of God's love in real relationships."[67] Men have a special calling before God that involves faithful and consistent leadership.

---

[66] Ron Schaeffer, *Blue Mountain Men's Camp* 30 April, 2001.

[67] Adapted in Richard Phillips, *The Masculine Mandate* (Lake Mary: Reformation Trust, 2010), 9.

Scripture sets forth the marching orders for men. One verse in 1 Corinthians spells out these orders with crystal clarity: "Be watchful, stand firm in the faith, act like men, be strong" (1 Cor. 16:13). In this passage, we will see four emerging imperatives that will prompt men to be men of conviction and courage. Each imperative will address four concerns:

1. *Meaning* - What does it mean?

2. *Motive* - Why carry out the imperative?

3. *Method* - Specific instructions for obeying the imperative.

4. *Model* - Christians who obeyed the imperative.

Imperative 1: Be Watchful

The *meaning* of the first imperative comes from the Greek word, *greigoréō*. The term means "to stay awake, stand alert, or to be aware of danger." The implication here is that Christians who are courageous and driven by conviction are vigilant; they avoid spiritual drowsiness.

In 1984, a commercial plane crashed in Spain. The investigators made an eerie discovery. The recording device or "black box" revealed that several minutes before impact a computer-generated voice from the plane's automatic warning system instructed the crew repeatedly in English, "Pull up! Pull up!" The pilot, evidently thinking the system was malfunctioning, snapped, "Shut up, Gringo!" and switched the system off. Minutes later, the plane crashed into the side of the mountain. Everyone on board perished.[68]

Watchful Christians stand guard. "Be sober-minded; be watchful. Your adversary the devil prowls around like a roaring lion, seeking someone to devour," writes the apostle in 1 Peter 5:8. Jesus warned his disciples, "Watch and pray that you may not enter into temptation. The spirit indeed is willing, but the

---

[68] See John F. MacArthur, *The Vanishing Conscience* (Dallas: Word Publishing, 1994), 36.

flesh is weak" (Matt. 26:41). We are called to "continue steadfastly in prayer, being watchful in it with thanksgiving" (Col. 4:2). And we watch for the return of our Savior: "Watch therefore, for you know neither the day nor the hour" (Matt. 25:13).

The *motives* for watchfulness are crucial. We have a propensity to grow lazy in the Christian life. It is so easy to let things slide. The command to remain watchful helps prevent spiritual sloth and spiritual drowsiness.

We remain watchful to avoid being taken captive. Paul warns the Colossian believers, "See to it that no one takes you captive by philosophy and empty deceit, according to human tradition, according to the elemental spirits of the world, and not according to Christ" (Col. 2:8). Such watchfulness involves a constant vigilance. Indeed, there are no breaks in the Christian life. We remain watchful to prevent being hauled off into a "spiritual gulag."

We remain watchful to steer clear from developing a hard heart: "Take care, brothers, lest there be in any of you an evil, unbelieving heart, leading you to fall away from the living God" (Heb. 3:12). Scripture warns, "Whoever hardens his heart will fall into calamity" (Prov. 28:14b). And we exercise watchfulness to avoid the snare of the world, the flesh, and the devil (1 John 2:15-16).

Two *methods* help us develop the discipline of watchfulness. First, learn to exercise biblical discernment. Learn to recognize theological and philosophical error. Scripture urges, "Do not be conformed to this world, but be transformed by the renewal of your mind, that by testing you may discern what is the will of God, what is good and acceptable and perfect" (Rom. 12:2). Followers of Christ must constantly be aware of their surroundings. They must constantly be on watch.

Tragically, discernment is declining in the church. False doctrine is regularly peddled from compromised pulpits. People in the pews are quick to accept theological nonsense. Itching ears are content with doctrinal drivel. When discernment declines, spinelessness gains momentum and weakens the church.

Solomon, while far from perfect, is a *model* of spiritual watchfulness. "Give your servant therefore an understanding mind to govern your people, that I may discern between good and evil, for who is able to govern this your great people?" (1 Kings 3:9). "And God said to him, 'Because you have asked this, and have not asked for yourself long life or riches or the life of your enemies, but have asked for yourself understanding to discern what is right ...'" (1 Kings 3:11). God's response in the next verse is decisive: " ... Behold, I give you a wise and discerning mind, so that none like you has been before you and none like you shall arise after you" (v. 12). Solomon was initially committed to watchfulness.[69] However, when idolatry gained the ascendency in his heart, he grew complacent and paid a heavy price for his laziness and disobedience.

Imperative 2: Stand Firm in the Faith

The *meaning* of this imperative comes from *steikō*. It is a present tense verb that means "to persevere, remain, or abide." The flavor here is to "hold the fort" and continually stand our ground. Dennis Rainey compares our responsibility with a soldier who stands his post at Arlington National Cemetery. This soldier stands with great resolve, even in the midst of adversity or during hurricane winds: "That's what a soldier does. He acknowledges the storm, but he doesn't give in to it. He stands firm." Rainey continues, "As a friend told me, "If these men can stand guard over the dead, how much more important is it that I stand guard over the living—my wife and my children?"[70] In the same manner, our responsibility is to stand firm in the faith, even when the crowd mocks us and when our accusers point the finger at us.

---

[69] See Brian Hedges, *Watchfulness: Recovering a Lost Spiritual Discipline* (Grand Rapids: Reformation Heritage Books, 2018).

[70] Dennis Rainey, *Stepping Up: A Call to Courageous Manhood*, 29-30.

Paul notes in Ephesians 6:14 that the proper posture for battle-ready saints is to *stand*. The term translated *stand* in this context means "to face or withstand something or someone with courage." It is translated various ways in the New Testament including "maintain, establish, or remain firmly." When we wear the whole armor of God, we are granted supernatural ability to *withstand* and *stand firm* (Eph. 6:12). "Therefore take up the whole armor of God, that you may be able to withstand in the evil day, and having done all, to stand firm" (Eph. 6:13). Ray Stedman adds, "The goal of the devil is always to produce discouragement, confusion, or indifference. Wherever we find ourselves victims of a state of confusion and uncertainty, or discouragement and defeat, or an indifferent and callous attitude toward life and others, we have already become prey to the wiles of the devil."[71]

What is the "evil day" that Paul refers to? First, it involves *an ungodly world*. Paul warns us about the *kósmos* in Colossians 2:8. "See to it that no one takes you captive by philosophy and empty deceit, according to human tradition, according to the elemental spirits of the world, and not according to Christ." He is referring to the pagan system that opposes God and his holy Word.

Second, it involves *an ungodly agenda*. Scripture describes the essence of this diabolical agenda:

> *But understand this, that in the last days there will come times of difficulty. For people will be lovers of self, lovers of money, proud, arrogant, abusive, disobedient to their parents, ungrateful, unholy, heartless, unappeasable, slanderous, without self-control, brutal, not loving good, treacherous, reckless, swollen with conceit, lovers of pleasure rather than lovers of God, having the appearance of godliness, but denying its power. Avoid such people (2 Tim. 3:1-5).*

Third, it involves *an ungodly enemy*. His name is Satan and is supported by an entourage of malicious demons. These satanic emissaries seek to threaten our faith, discourage our faith, and destroy us. These satanic ambassadors do the bidding of the

---

[71] Ray Stedman, *Spiritual Warfare* (Portland: Multnomah Press, 1975). 71.

prince of darkness. Their aim is to hinder the ministry (1 Thess. 2:18). They work with all their might to stir up pride in the people of God. For "pride goes before destruction, and a haughty spirit before a fall" (Prov. 16:18). Ultimately, their aim is to destroy the people of God. "The thief comes only to steal and kill and destroy ..." (John 10:10). We find the enemy working overtime to defeat God's people: "Simon, Simon, behold, Satan demanded to have you, that he might sift you like wheat" (Luke 22:31). After Satan tested Job and stripped him of his property and children, he attacked Job's health (Job 2:1-8).

It is in the face of this kind of satanic attack and opposition that we are called to stand firm. Such a posture is a commandment.[72] This is a settled resolution. This is a pre-commitment. Indeed, this is a mindset. In other words, before we enter the battlefield, we must embrace this resolution as a fact; we must *establish* this as a commitment in our hearts; we must be energized by this mindset. We must stand. When we stand, we are not only obeying God, we are banking on his strategy. And so we stand by faith! Notice six effects of *standing* in the life of Christians:

1. Standing signifies *seriousness*. The Christian life is serious business. As we have seen, we are engaged in war. Tragically, many Christians embrace a passive attitude which leads to a passive posture in the Christian life. A.W. Tozer laments, "Complacency is a deadly foe of all spiritual growth ...The shallowness of our inner experience, the hollowness of our worship, and that servile imitation of the world which marks our promotional methods all testify that we, in this day, know God only imperfectly, and the peace of God scarcely at all."[73] But followers of Christ know better. They understand the serious nature of the battle. And so their lives are marked by standing.

---

[72] The verb translated "stand" is written in the aorist active imperative.

[73] A.W. Tozer, *The Pursuit of God* (Camp Hill: Christian Publications, Inc. 1982), 17-18.

2. Standing signifies *steadfastness.* Christians who stand are prepared to fight. They are seasoned soldiers who are in it for the long haul. These soldiers are steadfast. Paul says that we stand in the gospel (1 Cor. 15:1). Peter says that we stand firm in the grace of God (1 Pet. 5:12).

3. Standing signifies *spiritual strength.* Paul encourages the young pastor, Timothy: "You then, my child be strengthened by the grace that is in Christ Jesus" (2 Tim. 2:1). *Strengthened* is an imperative that means "to be rendered more capable for a particular task." Spiritual soldiers need spiritual strength on a daily basis. Standing enables us to gain and maintain our spiritual strength.

4. Standing signifies *conviction.* A standing believer is a person of deep convictions that don't change with time or fade away when a new "sheriff" rides into town. A believer who stands is not detracted by the wind and waves of false teaching. Paul writes, " … until we all attain to the unity of the faith and of the knowledge of the Son of God, to mature manhood, to the measure of the stature of the fullness of Christ, so that we may no longer be children, tossed to and fro by the waves and carried about by every wind of doctrine, by human cunning, by craftiness in deceitful schemes" (Eph. 4:13–14).

5. Standing signifies *maturity.* Scripture reveals that when we stand, we remain watchful, which is a signpost to maturity: "Continue steadfastly in prayer, being watchful in it with thanksgiving" (Col. 4:2).

6. Standing signifies *hope.* The apostle Paul explains how this hope is ultimately grounded in Christ: "Through him we have also obtained access by faith into this grace in which we stand, and we rejoice in hope of the glory of God" (Rom. 5:2).

Notice two *motives* for standing firm in the faith. The first motive is negative; the second, positive. First, if we don't stand firm, we will get knocked down (Eph. 4:13-14). This devious doctrine is driven by "human cunning, by craftiness in deceitful schemes." If we don't stand firm, we will get knocked off our feet every time.

Second, we stand firm in the faith so that we might mature in the faith: "until we all attain to the unity of the faith and of the knowledge of the Son of God, to mature manhood, to the measure of the stature of the fullness of Christ ..." (Eph. 4:13). The word translated *mature* means "perfect," or "complete." It implies attaining a goal, in this case, Christian maturity. Paul uses the same term in Colossians 1:28. He writes, "Him, we proclaim, warning everyone and teaching everyone with all wisdom, that we may present everyone mature in Christ." We stand firm for the purpose of Christian maturity.

A biblical *model* of standing firm is the faithful saint, Polycarp. As the judge ordered him to cry, "Out with the atheists!" Polycarp responded by pointing to the crowd and saying, "Yes. Out with the atheists!" Again, the judge promised that if he would swear by the emperor and curse Christ, he would be free to go. But Polycarp replied, "For eighty-six years I have served him, and he has done me no evil. How could I curse my king, who saved me?"[74]

When the judge threatened to burn him alive, Polycarp simply answered that the fire about to be lit would only last a moment, whereas the eternal fire would never go out. After Polycarp was tied to the post in the pyre, he cast his gaze to the sky and prayed aloud: "Lord Sovereign God ... I thank you that you have deemed me worthy of this moment, so that, jointly with your martyrs, I may have a share in the cup of Christ ... For this ... I bless and glorify you."[75] Spinelessness had no place in Polycarp's vocabulary. He stood firm, even in the midst of horrifying persecution.

---

[74] Justo L. Gonzalez, *The Story of Christianity - Vol. 1* (San Francisco: Harper Collins Publishers, 1984), 44.

[75] Ibid.

Another biblical model of standing firm are the Hebrew stalwarts Shadrach, Meshach, and Abednego (Dan. 3:1-30). These faithful men stood strong through their fiery trial. First, they *stood firm when no one was looking.* In Daniel 3, we find the Chaldeans accusing Shadrach, Meshach, and Abednego. In the midst of their carnal finger-pointing, the Chaldeans address King Nebuchadnezzar: "You, O king, have made a decree, that every man who hears the sound of the horn, pipe, lyre, trigon, harp, bagpipe, and every kind of music, shall fall down and worship the golden image. And whoever does not fall down and worship shall be cast into a burning fiery furnace" (Dan. 3:10–11). The three men proved themselves faithful, even when the cameras weren't rolling. They understood the priority of standing firm in an ungodly world. They stood firm when no one was looking.

Second, *they stood firm when the king was fuming.* Daniel reports that Nebuchadnezzar was in a *furious rage.* The term comes from a Hebrew word that means "intense anger or wrath on an epic scale." The three men were ordered to report to the king. Nebuchadnezzar asked them, "Is it true, O Shadrach, Meshach, and Abednego, that you do not serve my gods or worship the golden image that I have set up? Now if you are ready when you hear the sound of the horn, pipe, lyre, trigon, harp, bagpipe, and every kind of music, to fall down and worship the image that I have made, well and good. But if you do not worship, you shall immediately be cast into a burning fiery furnace. And who is the god who will deliver you out of my hands?" (Dan. 3:14-15).

Notice how the courageous men respond to Nebuchadnezzar: "Shadrach, Meshach, and Abednego answered and said to the king, 'O Nebuchadnezzar, we have no need to answer you in this matter. If this be so, our God whom we serve is able to deliver us from the burning fiery furnace, and he will deliver us out of your hand, O king. But if not, be it known to you, O king, that we will not serve your gods or worship the golden image that you have set up.'" (Dan. 3:16–18). They stood firm, even in the midst of a fuming pagan king.

Third, *they stood firm when the fire was blazing*. When the men of bold resolve refused to bend the knee to Nebuchadnezzar and his pagan gods, the king's wrath was enraged even further. At which point, he ordered his servants to heat the furnace seven times hotter than usual and he cast the courageous men into the burning fiery furnace. But the story does not end in a mere puff of smoke. The Jewish men were bound and tossed into the blazing inferno where they would be incinerated on the spot. In fact, the Bible says that since Nebuchadnezzar ordered the furnace heated hotter, the flames killed the men who cast the prisoners into the burning blaze!

Daniel 3:24-25 describes what happened next: "Then King Nebuchadnezzar was astonished and rose up in haste. He declared to his counselors, "Did we not cast three men bound into the fire?" They answered and said to the king, "True, O king." He answered and said, "But I see four men unbound, walking in the midst of the fire, and they are not hurt; and the appearance of the fourth is like a son of the gods"" (Dan. 3:24–25).

When the men emerged from the fiery blaze, they were unscathed. Daniel 4:27 indicates that "the hair of their heads was not singed, their cloaks were not harmed, and no smell of fire had come upon them." Nebuchadnezzar's disposition was completed transformed. The man whose anger had been previously enflamed responded with kindness and respect: "Blessed be the God of Shadrach, Meshach, and Abednego, who has sent his angel and delivered his servants, who trusted in him, and set aside the king's command, and yielded up their bodies rather than serve and worship any god except their own god" (Dan. 4:28).

These men refused to back down in the face of unbelievable odds. They refused to cower before an ungodly king. They renounced the path of spinelessness that characterizes so many people. The key takeaway is this: People who stand firm trust in God. People who stand firm bank on the promises of God. They take God at his Word. Such an attitude fuels their resolve and enables obedient responses which honor the Lord.

Imperative 3: Be Courageous

The *meaning* of the third imperative is "be courageous" (CSB). The English Standard Version translates the Greek term, *ándridzomai* as "act like men." The term may be translated as "behaving with the wisdom and courage of a man - as opposed to a child in Christ." Strachan and Peacock observe, "Acting like a man means brave decision-making in order to exercise gracious lordship and dominion in his life ... Men take responsibility and initiative. They act. And they act in a way that marks mature manhood - courageous leadership. Where Adam was fearfully passive, true masculinity shows humble courage."[76] It means "to demonstrate courage in the face of danger." This man is anything but spineless. This man is bold and brave. He is lionhearted and valiant. He is unflinching and indomitable. He is ready to stand for Christ. This man is ready to proclaim the truth and is prepared to stand in the face of persecution.

An important *motive* for obeying this imperative is to flee from passivity, as we have already seen. Men are increasingly passive and cowardly. To speak in blunt terms, men are failing to pick up the mantel of leadership that God has entrusted us with. "Male passivity," writes Dennis Rainey, "is a disease that robs a man of his purpose while it destroys marriages, ruins families, and spoils legacies. A passive man doesn't engage, he retreats. He neglects personal responsibility. At its core, passivity is cowardice."[77]

Here is the bottom line: Men are either fleeing from passivity or they succumb to it. Passive men give in to the whims of culture and cater to carnality. Passive men are dominated by their wives and children. Such a man is spineless and fails to live up to God's divine standard.

Three specific *methods* help men obey this imperative. The first method for carrying out this imperative is rooted in the

---

[76] Owen Strachan & Gavin Peacock, *What Does the Bible Teach About Transgenderism?* (Geanies House, Fear, Ross-shire: Christian Focus Publication, 2020), 85.

[77] Dennis Rainey, *Stepping Up: A Call to Courageous Manhood*, 25.

first book of the Old Testament: "And the Lord God planted a garden in Eden, in the east, and there he put the man whom he had formed" (Gen. 2:8). Here we find man living according to God's covenantal mandate "in order to gain and act out his God-given identity there."[78] Genesis 2:15 provides the necessary framework: "The Lord God took the man and put him in the garden of Eden to work it and keep it." Richard Phillips adds, "That is the Masculine Mandate: to be spiritual men placed in the real-world, God-defined relationships, as lords and servants under God, to bear God's fruit by serving and leading."[79]

Second, we act like men by *working*. We are called to work in the "field" that God has placed us in. "Christian men should ... desire to cultivate something worthwhile for the glory of God and the well-being of their fellow men."[80] Christian men should cultivate human hearts. We should be in a position to influence, mentor, and disciple our children and people under our care (Eph. 6:4). Christian men should serve their wives (Eph. 5:25-30).

Third, we act like men by *keeping*. That is, we strive to protect and sustain progress in the world. The Hebrew term translated, *keep* means to "guard or protect." Therefore, we are called upon to protect those whom we nurture. We protect the people that God has charged us to shepherd.

The *model* for this imperative is the apostle Paul. Indeed, the apostle was the quintessential man. He was tough and tender. He was strong and self-effacing. He was committed to the covenantal model that follows the biblical pattern of working and keeping. One of the prime ways that Paul acted like a man was by maintaining an eternal perspective. Listen to his God-centered resolve in 2 Corinthians 4:16-18. The apostle writes, "So we do not lose heart. Though our outer self is wasting away, our inner self is being renewed day by day. For this light momentary affliction is preparing for us an eternal weight of glory beyond

[78] Phillips, *The Masculine Mandate*, 9.

[79] Ibid.

[80] Ibid, 13.

all comparison, as we look not to the things that are seen but to the things that are unseen. For the things that are seen are transient, but the things that are unseen are eternal."

Paul acted like a man in the marketplace. He acted like a man in the pulpit. He acted like a man when he settled disputes and mediated matters of controversy. And the apostle Paul acted like a man in his prayer closet. The courage that Paul displayed is a great example for anyone who seeks to steer clear from spineless living!

Imperative 4: Be Strong

The *meaning* of the fourth and final imperative in 1 Corinthians 16:13 comes from the Greek term, *krataioō* which is translated *be strong*. It means "to strengthen or establish." Paul uses the same term in his letter to the Ephesians: "… that according to the riches of his glory he may grant you to be *strengthened* with power through his Spirit in your inner being" (Eph. 3:16). Luke reveals that the Lord Jesus Christ "grew and became *strong*" (Luke 2:40). This is the kind of strength we seek to emulate.

The *motive* for this imperative is clear: God has appointed men to lead in the home and in the church. But the trend among American men is deeply troubling. The decline in masculine leadership is moving at an alarming rate.

In a recent Fox News series, Tucker Carlson addressed this disturbing trend away from masculine leadership. The series, "American Men Are in Crisis" reveals a shift in thinking among American men. Carlson reports, "This is a crisis. Yet our leaders pretend it's not happening … When men fail, all of us suffer." [81] The alarming note he sounds is clear and penetrating, yet very few appear to be listening.

Three *methods* will help us obey the imperative to *be strong*. First, *remember that the Lord reigns*. The psalmist reminds us that God is on the throne:

---

[81] http://dailycaller.com/2018/03/07/tucker-american-men-are-in-crisis-jordan-peterson/

The Lord reigns; he is robed in majesty; the Lord is robed; he has put on strength as his belt. Yes, the world is established; it shall never be moved. Your throne is established from of old; you are from everlasting. The floods have lifted up, O Lord, the floods have lifted up their voice; the floods lift up their roaring. Mightier than the thunders of many waters, mightier than the waves of the sea, the Lord on high is mighty! Your decrees are very trustworthy; holiness befits your house, O Lord, forevermore (Ps. 93:1–5).

When the Scriptures announce the reign of the Lord, this is an important way of declaring his kingship over all things:

Say among the nations, 'The Lord reigns! Yes, the world is established; it shall never be moved; he will judge the peoples with equity' (Ps. 96:10).

The Lord reigns, let the earth rejoice; let the many coastlands be glad! (Ps. 97:1).

The Lord reigns; let the peoples tremble! He sits enthroned upon the cherubim; let the earth quake! (Ps. 99:1).

The Lord has established his throne in the heavens, and his kingdom rules over all. (Ps. 103:19).

How beautiful upon the mountains are the feet of him who brings good news, who publishes peace, who brings good news of happiness, who publishes salvation, who says to Zion, 'Your God reigns' (Isa. 52:7).

Then I heard what seemed to be the voice of a great multitude, like the roar of many waters and like the sound of mighty peals of thunder, crying out, 'Hallelujah! For the Lord our God the Almighty reigns' (Rev. 19:6).

Abraham Kuyper adds, "In the total expanse of the human life, there is not a single square inch which Christ, who alone is sovereign, does not declare, 'That is mine.'"[82] God's kingly authority ushers in rejoicing; his kingly authority causes people to <u>tremble. Indeed,</u> God's kingly authority brings deep happiness

[82] Abraham Kuyper, *Sovereiniteit in Eigen Kring* (Amsterdam: J.H. Kruyt, 1880), 35. Cited in James Boice, *The Doctrines of Grace* (Wheaton: Crossway Books, 2002), 56.

and prompts courage in the downtrodden. C.H. Spurgeon underscores the comprehensive nature of God's reign:

> *Jehovah reigns. Whatever opposition may arise, his throne is unmoved; he has reigned, does reign, and will reign for ever and ever. Whatever turmoil and rebellion there may be beneath the clouds, the eternal King sits above all in supreme serenity; and everywhere he is really Master, let his foes rage as they may. All things are ordered according to his eternal purposes, and his will is done ... His is not the semblance but the reality of sovereignty. In nature, providence, and salvation the Lord is infinite in majesty.*[83]

GOD'S TRUTH ABIDETH STILL

When fear pounds at the door of your life - remember that Yahweh reigns. When your strength is gone - remember that Yahweh reigns. When evil persists—remember that Yahweh reigns. And when the "prophets" of postmodernity deride propositional truth—remember that Yahweh reigns. Indeed, as Luther rightly said, "God's truth abideth still!"

There is an indispensable need to acknowledge that the sovereign King reigns (Dan. 6:26) and that his control knows no boundaries; that he alone determines everything that comes to pass (Prov. 16:33: 21:1). We glory in the marvelous reality that our sovereign king does whatever he pleases (Ps. 115:3) and that he acts in order to advance his glory (Exod. 14:4). This sovereign God works all things according to the counsel of his will (Eph. 1:11). And we rest in the infinite wisdom of his plan, knowing that the purposes of this king can never be thwarted (Isa. 46:9-10; Job 42:2). For, "what God permits, he decrees to permit."[84]

When we set a high "spiritual bar," we proactively pursue a path of courage and conviction. When we obey the marching

---

[83] C.H. Spurgeon, *The Treasury of David* (Peabody: Hendrickson Publishers), 134.

[84] Jonathan Edwards, *Concerning the Divine Decrees* (Edinburgh: The Banner of Truth, 1934), 537.

orders set forth in 1 Corinthians 16:13, we jettison the path of spinelessness.

➤ 10 ➤

SETTLING THE MATTER OF WORLDVIEWS

—— ··· ——

"And we are soldiers – charged with pulling down ideolog-
ical strongholds and casting down the lies and deception
spawned by the forces of evil ... Our mission as soldiers
is to overthrow false ideas. We must keep those objectives
straight; we are not entitled to wage warfare against peo-
ple or to enter into diplomatic relations with anti-Chris-
tian ideas. Our warfare is not against flesh and blood and
our duty as ambassadors does not permit us to compromise
or align ourselves with any kind of human philosophies."[85]

John F. MacArthur

C hristians who live with courage and conviction must
settle the matter of worldviews. The term, *worldview*
was originally utilized by James Orr (1844-1913) in
order to present a systematic view of God and the world. Orr
shows how wide and encompassing this term is and how it
directly impacts our thinking:

> *He who with his whole heart believes in Jesus as the Son of*
> *God is thereby committed to much else besides. He is com-*
> *mitted to a view of God, to a view of man, to a view of*
> *sin, to a view of Redemption, to a view of human destiny,*

---

[85] John F. MacArthur, *The Truth War: Fighting for Certainty in an Age of*
Deception (Nashville: Thomas Nelson, 2007), 25.

found only in Christianity. This forms the 'Weltanschau-ung' or Christian view of the world.[86]

"A worldview," writes Ronald Nash, "is a set of beliefs about the most important issues of life. A worldview is a conceptual scheme by which we consciously or unconsciously place or fit everything we believe and by which we interpret and judge reality."[87] It is important to recognize that the human mind is not satisfied with pieces of knowledge that are unrelated. Therefore, worldviews are a powerful tool that help unpack how things really are. In other words, worldviews provide a framework for thinking about ultimate reality. David Naugle observes:

> *A philosophically sophisticated, God-centered conception of a Christian worldview spares believers from a naïve fideism, a scandalous anti-intellectualism, and a cultural obscurantism. In turn it imparts to them a cognitive confidence, an apologetic strategy, a cultural relevance, and a sound, spiritual basis for life in the coherent picture of God's larger story.*[88]

Worldviews show the stark contrast between biblical Christianity and false religious and philosophical systems. They help us see, as we observed above, how the pieces of knowledge fit together in a unified whole. My wife and mom enjoy working on puzzles together. Whenever they begin a new puzzle they dump hundreds of pieces on the kitchen table. At the beginning, it only looks like a jumbled mess. But after several hours (or days), the puzzle begins to take shape. It is miraculously transformed into a beautiful city scape or some other work of art. In the same way, worldviews help us see the big picture; they help us see things from God's vantage point.

Worldviews demonstrate the absolute lordship of Jesus Christ over all people and all things. Abraham Kuyper famously proclaims, "There is not a square inch in the whole domain of our

---

[86] James Orr, *The Christian View of God and the World* (Grand Rapids: Kregel, 1989 reprint), 4.

[87] Ronald H. Nash, *Worldviews in Conflict* (Grand Rapids: Zondervan, 1992), 16.

[88] David Naugle, *Worldview: History of a Concept* (Grand Rapids: Eerdmans Publishing Company, 2002), 9-10.

human existence over which Christ, who is Sovereign over all, does not cry, 'Mine.'"[89]

We live in a world where ideas compete for our attention on a daily basis. Pagan worldviews have the power to demoralize us and weaken our Christian resolve. A brief look at the last two hundred years reveals how the ideas of people influence our lives.

Charles Darwin (1809-1882)

Darwin authored *The Origin of Species* in 1859, which outline the theory of evolution where he maintains that all living organisms on earth descended from a single primordial form.

Karl Marx (1818-1883)

Marx maintained, "Religion is the sigh of the oppressed culture, the heart of a heartless world, and the soul of soulless conditions. It is the opium of the people."[90] His version of dialectical materialism asserts that "only matter exists."

Friedrich Nietzsche (1844-1900)

" … I call Christianity the one great curse … I call it the one immortal blemish of mankind."[91]

Sigmund Freud (1856-1939)

People invent religion out of a fear of nature. Freud argued, "God is a crutch for weak people."

NAVIGATING THE "GYPSY'S GRAVE"

There is something very interesting about these well-known

[89] Abraham Kuyper, "Sphere Sovereignty," in *Abraham Kuyper: A Centennial Reader*, ed. James D. Bratt (Grand Rapids: Eerdmans, 1998), 488.

[90] Marx and Engels, *Karl Marx-Frederick Engels: Collected Works*, vol. 3, 175. cited in David A. Noebel, *Understanding the Times* (Colorado Springs: Summit Ministries, 1995), 36.

[91] Friedrich Nietzsche, Cited in Stephen N. Williams, *The Shadow of the Antichrist* (Grand Rapids: Baker Academic, 2006), 13.

and pivotal thinkers. Each of these men continue to rule from the grave. The ideology and philosophy promoted during their earthly lives had a dominant effect on our culture. But these men continue to influence the fields of science, politics, philosophy, education, psychology, and even theology.

While each of these men were diverse and shared some very distinct views, it is important to understand that each of these men were atheists. Each of these thinkers repudiated the existence of God with a vengeance. The Word of God underscores the clear revelation of his existence in Romans 1:19-20. "For what can be known about God is plain to them, because God has shown it to them. For his invisible attributes, namely, his eternal power and divine nature, have been clearly perceived, ever since the creation of the world, in the things that have been made. So they are without excuse."

Additionally, Scripture describes the mindset of a person who repudiates the existence of God: "For although they knew God, they did not honor him as God or give thanks to him, but they became futile in their thinking, and their foolish hearts were darkened. Claiming to be wise, they became fools, and exchanged the glory of the immortal God for images resembling mortal man and birds and animals and creeping things" (Rom. 1:21–23). Carl Henry describes the consequences of this religious skepticism: "If modern man, the conqueror of outer space, does not make up his mind, he will vacillate intellectually to a gypsy's grave."[92]

For this reason, we must settle the matter of worldviews. As we shall soon discover, such a move will help equip our minds and enable our hands and feet to be a people of courage and conviction. Such a strategic move will move us far from the path of spinelessness.

What then, is our responsibility in a culture where pagan worldviews lock horns in a vicious battle for our hearts and

[92] Carl F.H. Henry, *God, Revelation and Authority: Volume 1* (Wheaton: Crossway Books, 1976), 43.

minds? Colossians 2:8 helps us move forward with God-centered courage and conviction: "See to it that no one takes you captive by philosophy and empty deceit, according to human tradition, according to the elemental spirits of the world, and not according to Christ." Notice three headings that emerge from this important verse:

THE CAUTION

Paul sounds the alarm in Colossians 2:8. It is as if he is the captain of a ship, crying out, "All hands-on deck. Danger is on the horizon. The iceberg is approaching. Warning! Beware! Be on alert!" Paul was not only warning the believers in the first-century Colossian church; he was warning us to beware of the spirit of the age.

The Significance Behind the Warning

The Greek term, *blepō* is translated as "see to it" (ESV), "be careful" (CSB), and "beware" (KJV). It means "to discern, perceive, or gaze." It means "to have the power of understanding; to weigh carefully; to examine." Paul writes in the imperative mood and calls the Colossians and all subsequent believers to exercise biblical discernment. Tim Challies reminds us, "Discernment is the skill of understanding and applying God's Word with the purpose of separating truth from error and right from wrong."[93]

There is an urgency included in this imperative. It would be much like floating the Amazon river and having your guide shout, "Watch out! Keep your hands out of the water. Beware of the piranhas!" The apostle Paul is warning the Colossians, "Watch out - keep your hands out of the water!" "See to it that no one takes you captive by philosophy and empty deceit, according to human tradition, according to the elemental spirits of the world, and not according to Christ" (Col. 2:8). Scripture utilizes the term *blepō* in several passages:

---

[93] Tim Challies, *The Discipline of Spiritual Discernment* (Wheaton: Crossway Books, 2008), 61.

Then Jesus replied to them: 'Watch out that no one deceives you' (Matt. 24:4, CSB).

Then Jesus began by telling them: 'Watch out that no one deceives you' (Mark 13:5, CSB).

Then He commanded them: 'Watch out! Beware of the yeast of the Pharisees and the yeast of Herod' (Mark 8:15, CSB).

In each passage, Jesus warns against spiritual deception; the same deception that we need to be aware of and guard against.

The Scriptures call us to maintain a discerning, watchful attitude at all times:

The wisdom of the prudent is to discern his way, but the folly of fools is deceiving (Prov. 14:8).

... and try to discern what is pleasing to the Lord (Eph. 5:10).

And it is my prayer that your love may abound more and more, with knowledge and all discernment, so that you may approve what is excellent, and so be pure and blameless for the day of Christ (Phil. 1:9-10).

With the alarm echoing in our hearts and minds, let us turn our attention from the caution to the concern.

THE CONCERN

The concern is "that no one take us captive." The term *captive* comes from *sulagōgeō* that means "to carry off as a spoil; to be seized or kidnapped." Paul is concerned that these believers who have been rescued from the domain of darkness (Col. 1:13) would become enslaved again and taken up in bondage (Gal. 5:1; 1 Pet. 1:14). Becoming a captive is a constant threat on the battlefield:

One of the most dangerous moments in combat in Europe in World War II came the instant a man decided he was no longer willing or able to continue combat. He threw down his weapon and raised his hands, or showed a white flag—sometimes alone, sometimes in a group, sometimes in company strength or even more—and thus exposed himself to an armed enemy soldier he had been trying to kill a moment before ... His chances of getting shot were high. They stayed high until he was safely in the rear of the POW cage.[94]

Is this not exactly where many Christians find themselves? Many of us have failed to heed Paul's warning. We have been deceived by the enemy. As a result, we are no longer willing to engage in combat. We find ourselves incarcerated in a self-imposed prison.

Are you a worldview POW? Have you given in to the musings of postmodern culture? Have you surrendered your weapon —the sword of the Spirit? Have you opted for the relative safety of the "POW cage?"

THE CREED

Explaining the Creed

We have learned that every culture has a set of dominant beliefs or principles which are articulated as a worldview. A worldview addresses a series of crucial questions such as: Who am I? What is my purpose? What is the meaning of life? What happens when I die? Does God exist? What is he like? How should I live? How can I determine right from wrong? How can I answer these questions? What is truth? And what or Who is the final authority?

A worldview is a set of core beliefs that influences that way we live our lives and the way we think. Every person has a worldview whether they realize it or not. For example, every person has a core belief about God (atheism, agnosticism, pantheism, panentheism, polytheism, monotheism, etc.).

---

[94] Stephen E. Ambrose, *Citizen Soldiers* (New York: Simon and Schuster, 1996), 351.

Articulating the Creed

Paul packs five terms into one sentence that describe the worldview he is warning about: " ... philosophy and empty deceit, according to human tradition, according to the elemental spirits of the world, and not according to Christ."

1. *Philosophy* - "love of wisdom."

2. *Empty* - "vain or devoid of the truth."

3. *Deceit* - "deceitfulness."

4. *Human tradition* - "that which has been handed down by men, namely, a creed or worldview which is characterized by empty deceit."

5. *Elemental spirits of the world* - "basic beliefs of false religious systems."

Paul is not warning against studying the discipline of philosophy; rather he is warning against any creed or worldview that is devoid of the truth, filled with deception, and fails to honor the Lord Jesus Christ as the supreme Creator and Sustainer of all things.

THE COLOSSIAN CREED AND THE CONTEMPORARY CREED

The two creeds that dominated the cultural landscape in Colossae were Judaism and Gnosticism. Judaism involved a mixture of Christianity, ceremonialism, legalism (2:16-17), mysticism (2:18-19), and asceticism (2:20-23).[95] Gnosticism, on the other hand, embraced a worldview that believed the body is evil and spirit is good. "Secret knowledge" is a key ingredient in this pagan worldview.

The contemporary creed that we see every day in our culture places a focus upon man's strength, man's will, man's ingenuity, man's creativity, and man's intellect. The contemporary creed focuses on experience and neglects doctrine. Salvation is a works-based scheme. The person, work, and deity of Christ are routinely

---

[95] See William Hendriksen, *Philippians, Colossians and Philemon* (Grand Rapids: Baker Book House, 1962), 109.

dismissed, mocked, or marginalized. And the authority of Scripture is cast aside.

Atheistic Naturalism

The reigning worldview is atheistic naturalism. Alistair McGrath says, "Atheism in its modern sense, has come to mean the explicit denial of all spiritual powers and supernatural beings, or the demand for the elimination of the transcendent as an illusion."[96]

Atheistic naturalism posits a universe with no Creator, no purpose, and no meaning. Nature is all that exists. Jean Paul Sartre, a well-known atheist writes, "Every existing thing is born without reason, goes on living out of weakness, and dies by accident."[97] Here, we find a worldview that mounts an aggressive frontal attack on supernaturalism where literally nothing is beyond the natural realm. The well-known atheist, Richard Dawkins adds, "I am attacking God, all gods, anything and everything supernatural, wherever and whenever they have been or will be invented."[98]

One of the refreshing aspects of atheistic naturalism is their brutal candor, which is typical in many proponents. For instance, Michael Ruse makes it clear that we are in a battle for ideas: "Evolutionists of all kinds must likewise work together to fight creationism."[99] One of the so-called horsemen of atheism, Daniel Dennett, acknowledges that atheism "eats through just about every traditional concept and leaves in its wake a revolutionized worldview."[100]

---

[96] Alistair McGrath, *The Twilight of Atheism* (New York: Doubleday, 2006), x.

[97] Jean Paul Sartre, cited in Robert Denoon Cumming, ed., *The Philosophy of Jean Paul Sartre* (New York: Random House, 1965), 66-67.

[98] Richard Dawkins, *The God Delusion* (Boston: Houghton Mifflin Company, 2006), 36.

[99] Michael Ruse, Cited in Ibid, 67.

[100] Daniel Dennett, cited in Nancy Pearcey, *Total Truth* (Wheaton: Crossway Books, 2004), 154.

HOW THEN, SHALL WE RESPOND?

This is precisely where spinelessness sets in among believers. Many Christians passively turn away from controversy and make this sobering lament: "These battles are fought in the university and in academic circles. Therefore, learning about worldviews and doing battle in the ideological realm does not have any relevance to me." Responses like this only breed cowardice and exacerbate this thorny dilemma.

So the reason for Paul's warning in Colossians 2:8 becomes clear. Our call is to be on guard against empty philosophical deception in our daily lives. John MacArthur warns, "To abandon biblical truth for empty philosophy is like returning to kindergarten after earning a doctorate."[101] We must, therefore, take the worldview warning seriously!

Paul warns us because false worldviews imprison people and turn our attention away from the whole point of Colossians - the preeminence and supremacy of the Lord Jesus Christ. Darwin, Marx, Nietzsche, Freud, and Sagan were worldview POW's because they began autonomously from themselves. They rejected God's revelation and ended up in a deep and damning hole.

Our responsibility is to carefully discern every ideology in order to avoid being captured as a worldview prisoner of war. Those committed to promoting Christ-less philosophy will pound on the castle door until we capitulate.

1. Resolve to never let them in.

2. Resolve to developing your Christian worldview for the glory of God.

3. Resolve to rejecting philosophy which does not glorify the Lord Jesus Christ.

4. Resolve to be a discerning person (1 Kings 3:9, 11).

5. Refuse to become a worldview prisoner of war.

---

[101] John F. MacArthur, *Colossians and Philemon* (Chicago: Moody Press, 1992), 102.

I urge you to strive to make a difference where God has placed you by speaking up for the truth, defending the truth, and contending for the truth.

SETTLING THE MATTER OF WORLDVIEWS

Perhaps this chapter led you to a frightening realization that you are trapped in a hole. You realize that you have been captured somewhere along the way by philosophy and empty deceit, according to human tradition, according to the elemental spirits of the world, and not according to Christ (Col. 2:8).

You need to understand that the Christian worldview is the only coherent worldview. "Only the Christian worldview is sufficient to answer the demands of secularization, nor can any other worldview provide the framework for true human flourishing."[102] The Christian faith is the only worldview that can be lived out consistently and meaningfully. As Nancy Pearcey writes, "Christianity fulfills both our reason and our spiritual yearnings."[103] The Bible tells us about one God who sent his Son to rescue prisoners of war (John 8:34). If you continue to live in your sin, you will pay a terrible price for that sin in the lake of fire where you will face the white-hot wrath of God.

The only way out of the hole is for Jesus Christ to drag you out! Because Jesus died on the cross for sinners and was raised up on the third day, he alone has the power to drag you out and forgive you of your sin (John 6:44). Is Jesus your Liberator? Ascending out of the abyss can never be achieved through your own flimsy efforts. You must trust in Christ alone! Cry out to him for freedom and forgiveness. And ask for the courage to bypass the spineless path.

[102] R. Albert Mohler, *The Gathering Storm: Secularism, Culture, and the Church* (Nashville: Nelson Books, 2020), 191.

[103] Nancy Pearcey, *Total Truth* (Wheaton: Crossway Books, 2004), 121.

⟫ 11 ⟨

SKETCHING A LINE IN THE SAND

— ••• —

*"Now there is no chance of recovery of preaching with-
out a prior recovery of conviction. We need to regain our
confidence in the truth, relevance and power of the gospel,
and begin to get excited about it again."*[104]

John R.W. Stott

Patrick Henry uttered these chilling words on March 23, 1775: "Give me liberty or give me death." A throng of men and women rallied around this battle cry, which led to the signing of the *Declaration of Independence*. Christians would do well to emulate the courage and conviction of this brave patriot. Simply put, we must be willing to stand up for our convictions. We must be prepared to don our spiritual armor and stand courageously in the marketplace of ideas. We must sketch a line in the sand.

The apostle Paul would have been impressed with Patrick Henry's sentiment. Once a slave to sin, Paul was miraculously transformed by Jesus Christ who died on a cross, was raised gloriously on the third day, and delivered him from "this present evil age" (Gal. 1:3). Jesus set him free and he was free indeed (John 8:36). And Paul rejoices in his new found liberty in Christ!

---

[104] John R.W. Stott, *Between Two Worlds: The Challenge of Preaching Today* (Grand Rapids: Eerdmans Publishing Company, 1982), 85.

Therefore, since we have been justified by faith, we have peace with God through our Lord Jesus Christ (Rom. 5:1).

We were buried therefore with him by baptism into death, in order that, just as Christ was raised from the dead by the glory of the Father, we too might walk in newness of life (Rom. 6:4).

There is therefore now no condemnation for those who are in Christ Jesus (Rom. 8:1).

For our sake he made him to be sin who knew no sin, so that in him we might become the righteousness of God (2 Cor. 5:21).

For freedom Christ has set us free; stand firm therefore, and do not submit again to a yoke of slavery (Gal. 5:1).

Paul shares the fighter's spirit and tenacity of men like Patrick Henry. When the gospel came under attack, Paul responds with courage and conviction. His rigorous defense of the gospel is on display in his letter to the Galatians. He defends his credentials as one who was called by Christ, conferred with authority, and commissioned as an apostle (Gal. 1:1-3). He confronts the Galatians for deserting the gospel and turning to a different gospel. He confronts false teachers and accuses these troublemakers of distorting the gospel (Gal. 1:6-7).

In Galatians 2, the Judaizers continue to assault the gospel with relentless force. Here we see the gospel on display, the gospel under attack, and the gospel affirmed.

THE GOSPEL IS ON DISPLAY

Then after fourteen years I went up again to Jerusalem with Barnabas, taking Titus along with me. I went up because of a revelation and set before them (though privately before those who seemed influential) the gospel that I proclaim among the Gentiles, in order to make sure I was not running or had not run in vain. But even Titus, who was with me, was not forced to be circumcised, though he was a Greek (Gal. 2:1–3).

The book of Acts indicates that Paul visited Jerusalem at least four times. Commentators are mixed as to whether Galatians 2 refers to Paul's second or third trip to Jerusalem. For our purposes, let us move our focus from the timing of the events to the actual event itself.

Three men arrive in Jerusalem, Paul and Barnabas—both Jews, and Titus who was Greek (remember Greeks were not circumcised). Paul explains that the reason for the trip was "because of a revelation." In other words, God directed him to go. Why would God send two Jews and a Greek to the heart of Jerusalem? I believe God sent these men to Jerusalem to put the gospel on display.

Paul has labored to help the Galatians understand that sinners may stand innocent in the sight of God by grace alone through faith alone. So he stands side-by-side with Timothy, an uncircumcised Christ-follower in a Jewish culture. Remember the importance and significance of circumcision to the Jews (Gen. 17:9-14). Ever since Genesis 17, the removal of the male foreskin had been the defining mark of the people of God. This mark indicated whether or not a person was inside or outside the covenant.

The apostles did not force Titus to be circumcised. That is, there was no disparity between Paul's gospel and the gospel of the other apostles. But the Judaizers wanted people to see that there was a "contradiction" between Paul and the apostles in Jerusalem. Timothy stands in as an object lesson for the truth of the gospel. His example teaches us a lesson that we learn later in Paul's letter to the Galatian believers: "For in Christ Jesus neither circumcision nor uncircumcision counts for anything, but only faith working through love" (Gal. 5:6).

This narrative teaches us an important lesson that have a bearing on courage and conviction. *We must stand secure because of who we are in Christ.* It must have been intimidating at one level for Titus to stand before a group of Jews as an uncircumcised man. It only takes one moment to step outside the realm of a gospel-centered life. But Titus recognized his identity in Christ. He understood that God accepted him on the basis of what Christ accomplished on his behalf—nothing more and nothing less! We are complete in Christ.

Titus beautifully displayed the gospel as he stood before the apostles in Jerusalem. He was accepted on the basis of Christ's completed work on the cross. But not everyone was happy when they learned that an uncircumcised man was in their midst.

THE GOSPEL IS ATTACKED

> *Yet because of false brothers secretly brought in—who slipped in to spy out our freedom that we have in Christ Jesus, so that they might bring us into slavery—to them we did not yield in submission even for a moment, so that the truth of the gospel might be preserved for you (Gal. 2:4–5).*

A *false brother* (*pseudádelphos*) is an individual who pretends to be a member of a particular group. Paul includes *false brothers* among the list of dangerous things that he faced in 2 Corinthians 11:22-27. These hooligans slipped in secretly as Galatians 2:4 indicates. [105] The Galatian church was not the only body of believers that dealt with these hucksters. Jude faced them as well: "For certain people have crept in unnoticed who long ago were designated for this condemnation, ungodly people, who pervert the grace of our God into sensuality and deny our only Master and Lord, Jesus Christ" (Jude 4).

False teachers use stealth, that is, they creep into the church and nobody even notices. They fly under the radar and use deceptive means to accomplish their mission. The mission of the false teachers in Galatia was clear. Paul says their goal was to bring God's people into bondage. In particular, they were mandating that Gentiles get circumcised, which would render the Christ-follower a slave to his former way of life.

---

[105] "Secretly" comes from the Greek term, *pareisaktos* which means "to join under false pretenses."

Whenever you add a condition to grace, you become a slave to that condition. Remember, when you abandon the gospel, you abandon Christ!

Paul's response is filled with courage and conviction: "...To them we did not yield in submission even for a moment, so that the truth of the gospel might be preserved for you." (Gal. 2:5). Paul says in effect, "I will not abandon the gospel!"

In his popular novel, *East of Eden*, the American author, John Steinbeck observes, "At such a time it seems natural and good to me to ask myself these questions. What do I believe in? What must I fight for and what must I fight against?"[106] These are the kinds of questions that every follower of Christ must face. But we must do more than merely face the question. We must stand with courage and conviction when false teachers threaten the purity of the gospel. Five principles will help us sketch a line in the sand.

First, *rise up and stand guard against the enemies of the gospel.* Paul warned the Ephesian elders:

> *Pay careful attention to yourselves and to all the flock, in which the Holy Spirit has made you overseers, to care for the church of God, which he obtained with his own blood. I know that after my departure fierce wolves will come in among you, not sparing the flock; and from among your own selves will arise men speaking twisted things, to draw away the disciples after them (Acts 20:28–30).*

It is time for men, in particular, to flee from passivity and guard the families that have been entrusted to them. It is time for male elders to be vigilant and guard the flocks that God has entrusted to our care. It is time to rise up and stand guard against the enemies of the gospel.

Second, *remember, the gospel is not a truth. The gospel is the truth.* Richard Phillips observes, "The gospel is not merely another meta narrative; it is the *true metanarrative*. It is the true

---

[106] John Steinbeck, *East of Eden* (New York: Penguin Books, 1952), 131.

story that God tells about what God has done so that we will know what to believe and how to behave."[107] It is a sobering thought to realize that "nine percent of evangelical students say that they believe in absolute truth."[108] Let's remember an important fact: There is no disparity between Paul's gospel, Peter's gospel, and Jesus's gospel. They all preach one gospel. They all preach the same gospel!

Francis Schaeffer spoke often about true Truth. Truth with a capital T. Despite the unity of truth claims in the Scripture, evangelicals are turning their backs on the authority of Scripture. "The fundamental retreat from the authority of Scripture is in large measure an offshoot of the Enlightenment," writes D.A. Carson.[109] Os Guinness adds, "Contemporary evangelicals are no longer people of the truth."[110]

- We grow uncomfortable drawing dogmatic lines in the sand.
- We begin to accept erroneous theological propositions.
- We grow weary of defending the Bible.
- We begin to get comfortable with religious pluralism.

Martin Lloyd-Jones confronts the spinelessness that characterizes many churches:

> *There can be little doubt but that the Church is as she is today because we do not follow the New Testament teaching and its exhortations, and confine ourselves to the positive and the so-called 'simple-gospel,' and fail to stress the negatives and the criticism. The result is that people do not recognize error when they meet it.*[111]

Lloyd-Jones continues:

---

[107] Richard Phillips, Ed. *Only One Way?* (Wheaton: Crossway Books, 2006), 99.

[108] Ibid, 84.

[109] D.A. Carson, *The Gagging of God* (Grand Rapids: Zondervan Publishing House, 1996), 363.

[110] Os Guinness, Cited in Richard Phillips, *Only One Way?*, 84.

[111] Martyn Lloyd-Jones, Cited in Ibid, 358.

It is not pleasant to be negative; it is not enjoyable to have to denounce and expose error. But any pastor who feels in little measure, and with humility, the responsibility for which the Apostle Paul knew in an infinitely greater degree for the souls and well-being spirituality of his people is compelled to utter these warnings. It is not liked and appreciated in this modern flabby generation.[112]

Third, *renew our commitment to the truth of the gospel.* Paul reminds us that the church is "a pillar and buttress of the truth" (1 Tim. 3:15). Instead of compromising the truth, we renew our commitment to the truth. We do not trifle with the truth. And as we renew our commitment to the truth of the gospel, we stand with Jude who urged the first century believers to "contend for the faith that was once for all delivered to the saints" (Jude 3).

Fourth, *refuse to capitulate to the grace robbers.* The grace robbers that Paul faced were experts at twisting and manipulating the truth. But Paul refused to budge: "We did not yield in submission even for a moment, so that the truth of the gospel might be preserved for you" (Gal. 2:5). John Stott adds, "The Christian has been set free from the law in the sense that his acceptance before God depends entirely upon God's grace in the death of Jesus Christ received by faith. To introduce the works of the law and make our acceptance depend on our obedience to rules and regulations was to bring a free man into bondage again."[113]

Finally, *resolve to stand on Christ alone and for Christ alone.* False teachers, theological hucksters, and heretics will go to great lengths to discourage and dismantle the people of God. Our task is to stay true to our Savior and draw a bold line in the sand. Scripture reminds us, "And because of him you are in Christ Jesus, who became to us wisdom from God, righteousness and sanctification and redemption ..." (1 Cor. 1:30).

As followers of Jesus, we are called to stand *on* Christ alone:

---

[112] Ibid.

[113] John R.W. Stott, *The Message of Galatians* (Downers Grove: Intervarsity Press, 1968), 43.

"So then you are no longer strangers and aliens, but you are fellow citizens with the saints and members of the household of God, built on the foundation of the apostles and prophets, Christ Jesus himself being the cornerstone, in whom the whole structure, being joined together, grows into a holy temple in the Lord" (Eph. 2:19-21). Christ is our Rock. He alone is our fortress. In him, we find refuge. He is the source of our salvation. As followers of Jesus, we are called to stand *for* Christ alone.

THE GOSPEL IS AFFIRMED

And from those who seemed to be influential (what they were makes no difference to me; God shows no partiality) — those, I say, who seemed influential added nothing to me. On the contrary, when they saw that I had been entrusted with the gospel to the uncircumcised, just as Peter had been entrusted with the gospel to the circumcised (for he who worked through Peter for his apostolic ministry to the circumcised worked also through me for mine to the Gentiles), and when James and Cephas and John, who seemed to be pillars, perceived the grace that was given to me, they gave the right hand of fellowship to Barnabas and me, that we should go to the Gentiles and they to the circumcised. Only, they asked us to remember the poor, the very thing I was eager to do (Gal. 2:6–10).

The apostles affirm Paul's message by giving him the right hand of fellowship. When the message is affirmed, it continues to advance. Some go to the Gentiles (uncircumcised). Some go to the Jews (circumcised). Whenever the gospel advances, good things happen. Hospitals and homes are built. Hungry people are fed. The poor are clothed. Addictions are conquered. Sinful habits are broken. People are made right with God, their sins are forgiven, their lives are transformed, and ministries of mercy are carried out.

THE RALLY CRY OF COURAGE AND CONVICTION

When Paul comes face-to-face with false teachers and deceivers, he sketches a line in the sand. Truth is on the line. The gospel is at stake. What about you? Where do you need to draw the line in the sand? Where do you need to establish boundaries that clearly reflect God's plan for the ages?

When the gospel is attacked, we must stand our ground and refuse to yield to grace robbers! May we faithfully take the gospel to the people that God has called us to minister to. May we draw a line in the sand by displaying the gospel, defending the gospel, and declaring the gospel to every tribe and nation! May our cry be, "Give us liberty or give us death!" May we grow strong in our doctrinal convictions as we spread the gospel message to every people group for the glory of God. And may we steer clear from the spineless path.

≫ 12 ≪

STANDING COURAGEOUSLY FOR THE TRUTH

— ••• —

"'Courage, dear heart'," and the voice, she felt sure, was Aslan's and with the voice a delicious smell breathed in her face."[114]

C.S. Lewis

The apostle John saw a wonderful sight and left us a record of his vision in the fifth chapter of the book of Revelation: "And they sang a new song, saying, 'Worthy are you to take the scroll and to open its seals, for you were slain, and by your blood you ransomed people for God from every tribe and language and people and nation, and you have made them a kingdom and priests to our God, and they shall reign on the earth'" (Rev. 5:9–10). John understood the redemptive purposes of God. He understood the salvific plan of the sovereign Savior. And John understood the necessity of standing courageously for the truth.

Like John, the apostle Paul was an exemplar of gospel proclamation. From the early days of his miraculous conversion to the moment before he breathed his last breath, Paul was fixated on the gospel. The gospel governed his thoughts. The gospel

---

[114] C.S. Lewis, *The Voyage of the Dawn Treader*, The Chronicles of Narnia (New York: HarperCollins, 2000), 187.

governed his aspirations. It governed his ethics. It governed his worldview. The gospel of Jesus Christ governed his life.

Can the same be said about you? Does the gospel govern your thoughts? Or, has the world taken your thoughts captive? Does the gospel govern your aspirations? Or, has our postmodern culture duped you into living a life that stands in opposition to God's Word? Does the gospel govern your ethics? Or, has the worldly system tricked you into embracing the pagan notion of relativism? Does the gospel govern your worldview? Or, have you been seduced by the spirit of the age? And does the gospel govern your life? Or have you been duped? Have you been deceived? In short, are you numbered among the spineless?

In his letter to the church in Rome, Paul stood his ground. In doing so, he modeled biblical courage and conviction for the first-century believers. This Spirit-enabled courage and conviction not only emboldened the Roman Christ-followers; it serves to strengthen us now, especially in our age of tolerance and relativism. Paul says, "For I am not ashamed of the gospel, for it is the power of God for salvation to everyone who believes, to the Jew first and also to the Greek" (Rom. 1:16). There is no fear in the apostle . His mind is resolute. His heart is filled with courage and conviction. His hands and feet bear witness to his God-centered valor.

THE CONTEXT OF THE GOSPEL

It is said that "context is king." The context of the gospel, then, is the stark black backdrop of sin. *The Westminster Confession of Faith* provides six helpful snapshots.[115]

1. Our first parents, being seduced by the subtilty and temptation of Satan, sinned, in eating the forbidden fruit. This their sin, God was pleased, according to his wise and holy counsel, to permit, having purposed to order it to his own glory.

---

[115] G.I. Williamson, Ed. *The Westminster Confession of Faith* (Phillipsburg: Presbyterian & Reformed Publishing, 2004), 69-80.

2. By this sin they fell from their original righteousness and communion with God, and so became dead in sin, and wholly defiled in all the parts and faculties of soul and body.

3. They being the root of all mankind, the guilt of this sin was imputed; and the same death in sin, and corrupted nature, conveyed to all their posterity descending from them by ordinary generation.

4. From this original corruption, whereby we are utterly indisposed, disabled and made opposite to all good, and wholly inclined to all evil, do proceed all actual transgressions.

5. This corruption of nature, during this life, doth remain in those that are regenerated; and although it be, through Christ, pardoned, and mortified; yet both itself, and all the motions thereof, are truly and properly sin.

6. Every sin, both original and actual, being a transgression of the righteous law of God, and contrary thereunto, doth, in its own nature, bring guilt upon the sinner, whereby he is bound over to the wrath of God, and curse of the law, and so made subject to death, with all miseries spiritual, temporal, and eternal.

In order to understand the gospel, we must first understand its context. If we don't understand that we have inherited a sinful nature from our father, Adam, we will have no need for the gospel. If we don't grasp that apart from grace we are dead in sin, we will have no need for the gospel. If we don't see that we lost the capacity to serve God or please him apart from grace, we have no need for the gospel. If we don't realize that we are under the wrath of God, we have no need for the gospel. If we don't comprehend that we are on the fast track to hell and that we will bear the weight of all our sin for ever and ever, we have no need for the gospel (1 Cor. 1:18).

As followers of Christ who are growing in courage and conviction, we need to tell people about the context of the gospel. We need to abandon the sidelines and shake off our fears and insecurities. People desperately need to hear and understand their lost condition apart from grace and without Christ.

> *Therefore, just as sin came into the world through one man, and death through sin, and so death spread to all men because all sinned— (Rom. 5:12).*

> *And you were dead in the trespasses and sins in which you once walked, following the course of this world, following the prince of the power of the air, the spirit that is now at work in the sons of disobedience— among whom we all once lived in the passions of our flesh, carrying out the desires of the body and the mind, and were by nature children of wrath, like the rest of mankind (Eph. 2:1–3).*

> *Whoever believes in the Son has eternal life; whoever does not obey the Son shall not see life, but the wrath of God remains on him (John 3:36).*

With a better understanding of the context of the gospel, look next at the content of the gospel.

THE CONTENT OF THE GOSPEL

Meaning

The *euangélion*, or the gospel, is best described as the good news. It is the heart-warming and soul-stirring revelation that Jesus has broken into our world and offers salvation through his life, death, and resurrection from the dead. Paul spoke in plain terms about this gospel: "Now I would remind you, brothers, of the gospel I preached to you, which you received, in which you stand, and by which you are being saved, if you hold fast to the word I preached to you—unless you believed in vain. For I delivered to you as of first importance what I also received: that Christ died for our sins in accordance with the Scriptures" (1 Cor. 15:1–3).

The gospel is the good news that was promised in Genesis 3:15. The gospel is the good news that Abraham received when God made an earth-shaking promise in Genesis 12:2-3. "And I will make of you a great nation, and I will bless you and make your name great, so that you will be a blessing. I will bless those who bless you, and him who dishonors you I will curse, and in you all the families of the earth shall be blessed."

The gospel begins with God who is holy, holy, holy (Hab. 1:13; Exod. 34:6-7). God the Father sent his Son, the Lord Jesus Christ to redeem a people for his own possession (1 Pet. 2:9). All people are sinners by nature and choice and are under the holy judgment and wrath of God (Rom. 5:12; John 3:36). Christ is fully God and fully man. He died on the cross for the sins of everyone who would ever believe. And God raised him from the dead on the third day (1 Tim. 1:15; 2:5; Rom. 4:25). God not only *invites* all people; he *commands* them to turn from their sin and believe in Christ alone for their eternal salvation (Acts 16:31).

Magnitude

This gospel began in Jerusalem and spread to Judea and Samaria and to the ends of the earth (Acts 1:8). This gospel would be an unstoppable force in the lives of each of one of God's elect.

In Acts 28:28-31 Paul proclaims, "Therefore let it be known to you that this salvation of God has been sent to the Gentiles; they will listen." He lived there two whole years at his own expense, and welcomed all who came to him, proclaiming the kingdom of God and teaching about the Lord Jesus Christ with all boldness and without hindrance." This gospel, then, is the only hope for sinners! Nothing more, nothing less. This means that sinners can never rely on their works. Sinners cannot rely on their wisdom. They can't rely on their brains. They can't rely on their brawn. This gospel is the only *lifeline* they have. Christ is the answer!

THE CONCERN OF THE GOSPEL

Paul writes, "For I am not ashamed of the gospel" (Rom. 1:16). This raises an important question: Why would anyone be ashamed of the gospel in the first place? The Greek term translated "ashamed" refers to someone who is characterized by feelings of shame, guilt, or embarrassment. When it comes to the gospel, then, there are two major concerns that may cause such shame.

Ashamed of a Proposition

The gospel is in fact, a proposition as we have seen. Yet this is precisely where some show signs of shame. There are several ways that the propositional truth of the gospel may cause shame to surface.

First, this is an *exclusive gospel*. The gospel posits a distinctly Christian worldview. By definition, this gospel requires people to believe in one God who reveals himself in three persons. This gospel requires people to believe in the 66 books, which are God-breathed, without error in the original autographs, infallible, and authoritative. This gospel requires sinners to believe in one Savior, the God-man, Jesus Christ who died for them on a cross and rose again on the third day.

Second, this is a *narrow gospel*. Jesus spoke about this narrow gospel in his high priestly prayer to the Father. He says, "And this is eternal life, that they know you the only true God, and Jesus Christ whom you have sent" (John 17:3).

Third, this is a *dogmatic gospel*. This gospel has no room for competitors. It has no room for other religious leaders or movements. Religious pluralism simply fails to pass the test that is required by the gospel. Indeed, it is a dogmatic gospel.

Fourth, this is an *uncompromising gospel*. The claims that Jesus makes are indisputable and require complete and total allegiance. Such a claim should not come as a surprise as Paul regularly refers to himself as a slave to the Lord Jesus Christ.

Ashamed of a Person

But the propositional truth of the gospel is not the only thing causes shame. Some people are ashamed of a Person. This Person is holy, holy, holy. This Person makes specific demands. This Person makes judgments. Jesus challenges sinners to turn from their sin. He calls them to holiness.

Additionally, Jesus makes challenging assertions. He says:

> *I am the vine; you are the branches. Whoever abides in me and I in him, he it is that bears much fruit, for apart from me you can do nothing (John 15:5).*

> *If anyone does not abide in me he is thrown away like a branch and withers; and the branches are gathered, thrown into the fire, and burned (John 15:6).*

> *If you keep my commandments, you will abide in my love, just as I have kept my Father's commandments and abide in his love (John 15:10).*

> *And he said to all, 'If anyone would come after me, let him deny himself and take up his cross daily and follow me' (Luke 9:23).*

THE CONSEQUENCES OF BEING ASHAMED OF THE GOSPEL

Jesus clearly describes the consequences of being ashamed of the gospel in Mark 8:38. "For whoever is ashamed of me and of my words in this adulterous and sinful generation, of him will the Son of Man also be ashamed when he comes in the glory of his Father with the holy angels."

Paul the apostle understands the stakes here. In Romans 1:16, he writes, "For I am not ashamed of the gospel ..." Paul is not sheepish. Paul is not apologetic. Paul does not make excuses. He never back-peddles. There is no equivocation in this man. He says, "I am not ashamed of the gospel." How could anyone be ashamed of such a wonderful gospel and such a wonderful Savior? How could anyone be spineless?

COWARDICE OR COURAGE?

As we draw this chapter to a close, think carefully and deeply. When we understand the consequences of being ashamed of Jesus and his gospel, it leaves us in a very precarious position. If we are honest, we have all been there. We have all fallen prey to cowardice. We have all been spineless. Even the apostle Peter struggled for a season with being ashamed of Jesus:

> Now Peter was sitting outside in the courtyard. And a servant girl came up to him and said, 'You also were with Jesus the Galilean.' But he denied it before them all, saying, 'I do not know what you mean.' And when he went out to the entrance, another servant girl saw him, and she said to the bystanders, 'This man was with Jesus of Nazareth.' And again he denied it with an oath: 'I do not know the man.' After a little while the bystanders came up and said to Peter, 'Certainly you too are one of them, for your accent betrays you.' Then he began to invoke a curse on himself and to swear, 'I do not know the man.' And immediately the rooster crowed. And Peter remembered the saying of Jesus, 'Before the rooster crows, you will deny me three times.' And he went out and wept bitterly (Matt. 26:69–75).

What causes a person to grow ashamed of the most important Person who brought the most important message? Several factors may play a role in the formation of cowardice:

First, *a mind which is clouded by the world's system.*

> Do not love the world or the things in the world. If anyone loves the world, the love of the Father is not in him. For all that is in the world—the desires of the flesh and the desires of the eyes and pride of life—is not from the Father but is from the world. And the world is passing away along with its desires, but whoever does the will of God abides forever (1 John 2:15–17).

John's imperative to "stop loving the world or the things in the world" strikes at the core of a cowardly person. As one is drawn into the web of the worldly system, he or she grows weaker and progressively loses any semblance of Christian courage. The world's system has a way of draining courage and replacing it with a dependence on its ungodly ideals.

Second, *a heart which is hardened by the deceitfulness of sin.* The writer of Hebrews warns, "Take care, brothers, lest there be in any of you an evil, unbelieving heart, leading you to fall away from the living God. But exhort one another every day, as long as it is called 'today,' that none of you may be hardened by the deceitfulness of sin" (Heb. 3:12-13). Several observations will enable us to see what this passage is driving at.

To begin with, the author writes in the imperative mood. *Take care (blépō)* is a word that occurs frequently in the New Testament and sometimes designates a warning. Such is the case here as believers are exhorted to steer clear of an evil heart of unbelief.

Next, the writer strategically stacks his words in order to show the tragic consequences of sin. *Evil* and *unbelieving* are diabolical characteristics that develop over time in the heart. These inclinations always lead to a tragic end, namely, falling away from the living God.

The passage clearly describes the correlation between an evil, unbelieving heart and reveals how over time a hardening sets in. Consider a patient who refuses to care for his body and ends up in the hospital with hardened arteries and cardiac arrest. In a similar way, when sin and unbelief go unchecked, they build up over time, leading to a hardened heart which contributes to the onset of cowardice.

Third, *priorities that are misaligned.* "And he said to all, 'If anyone would come after me, let him deny himself and take up his cross daily and follow me. For whoever loses his life for my sake will save it. For what does it profit a man if he gains the whole world and loses or forfeits himself'" (Luke 9:23-25). When we turn aside from the narrow path that Jesus commands, we turn inward and our courage evaporates. The sinful and selfish path that so many travel upon is the path of cowardice.

Many Christian men, in particular, have strayed far from the path of God's standard. Scripture specifically focuses on the responsibility of men: "Be watchful, stand firm in the faith, act like men, be strong. Let all that you do be done in love" (1 Cor. 16:13–14). Owen Strachan and Gavin Peacock observe, "Acting like a man means brave decision-making in order to exercise gracious lordship and dominion in his life ... Men take responsibility and initiative. They act. And they act in a way that marks mature manhood-courageous leadership. Where Adam was fearfully passive, true masculinity shows humble courage."[116] Instead of standing courageously, a host of Christian men have priorities that are misaligned; they stand passively on the sidelines like their father, Adam.

Fourth, *a life that has been taken captive by worldly philosophy.* Scripture warns, "See to it that no one takes you captive by philosophy and empty deceit, according to human tradition, according to the elemental spirits of the world, and not according to Christ" (Col. 2:8). Once again, the term blépō is utilized and translated as "see to it." The warning here is a stern one, as Paul urges the Colossian believers to steer clear from worldly philosophies and worldviews that run counter to historic Christianity. Whenever we become ensnared by worldly philosophy, our courage is crushed and cowardice gains momentum in our lives.

THE CURE FOR COWARDICE

We have explored the importance of courage and have seen several aspects of cowardice. The cure for the deadly disease of cowardice is repentance. God is calling his people to turn from the world's system. He is calling his people to turn from the deceitfulness of sin. God is calling his people to turn in such a way that our priorities are in alignment with kingdom priorities.

[116] Owen Strachan and Gavin Peacock, *What Does the Bible Teach About Transgenderism?* (Geanies House, Fear, Ross-shire: Christian Focus Publications, 2020), 85.

Indeed, our priorities should be in step with our sovereign Savior! And God is calling his people to turn away from man-made philosophy. Now is the time for action. Now is the time to turn from spinelessness!

STEADFAST CONVICTIONS

"May we never care what men say of us, so long as we walk in the light of God's Word. May we strive and pray to be wholly independent of, and indifferent to man's opinion, so long as we please God."[117]

J.C. Ryle

Richard Baxter (1615-1691) was a dominant figure in the seventeenth-century British landscape. Ordained into the church of England at the age of 23, Baxter was a faithful preacher who sought to maintain peace among people. He was fond of the popular line by Rupertus Meldenius: "In essentials unity, in non-essentials liberty, in all things charity."[118]

Baxter's aim for unity was tempered by his love of orthodoxy, which ultimately led him to declare himself as a "Nonconformist." As many godly men have discovered, such a position draws ire from critics on both sides of the aisle. Baxter refused to sway and captivated expositors in every generation with his

---

[117] J.C. Ryle, *Warnings to the Churches* (Edinburgh: The Banner of Truth Trust, 1967), 37.

[118] See Mark Ross, [] https://www.ligonier.org/learn/articles/essentials-unity-non-essentials-liberty-all-things/.

well-known words, "I preached as never sure to preach again, and as a dying man to dying men."

Any Christian leader who is willing to make a bold stand for the sake of the gospel *will face opposition*. Any Christian leader who dares to preach dogmatic doctrinal propositions and draw non-negotiable lines in the sand is bound to end up in hot water somewhere along the line. Jonathan Edwards' convictions got him fired. William Tyndale's convictions led him to the pyre where he was burned at the stake. John Bunyan's convictions got him thrown in jail. Martin Luther's convictions led to a lifelong bounty that stalked him to his dying day. And the apostle Paul's convictions cost him his life.

Any Christian leader who raises the banner of truth and has the audacity to cling to a set of convictions, especially doctrinal convictions, will inevitably be accused of having an "agenda." Such leaders are looked upon with derision and suspicion. Yet, each of the Christian leaders noted above, truly had a clear agenda.

The apostle Paul's agenda was centered around the gospel of Jesus Christ. Paul's agenda was the motivating factor in his life. This agenda fueled his resolve. This agenda was activated by his hands and feet. It dictated every decision and every dream. Paul's gospel agenda includes two mammoth pillars, immovable pillars that weather every storm and withstand every trial. His agenda was to *proclaim Christ* and *present everyone mature in Christ*.

PROCLAIM CHRIST

Paul writes to the Colossian believers, "Him we proclaim, warning everyone and teaching everyone with all wisdom, that we may present everyone mature in Christ" (Col. 1:28). This ministry of proclamation involves three mighty realties.

Strong Proclamation

Proclaim (ESV, NAS, CSB), or *preach* (KJV) is the English translation of *katangéllō*, which means "to declare plainly, openly, and aloud; to announce; to celebrate." The term is not limited to the ministry of formal preaching, however. When God sovereignly drew my wife (who was unknown by me, at the time), to receive the free gift of salvation, her youth pastor simply shared the gospel and asked, "Is there any reason why you wouldn't put your trust in Christ today?" His timely question was a powerful means of proclamation that my wife will never forget. Strong proclamation takes place in pulpits, classrooms, locker rooms, and coffee shops. Strong proclamation will be found around dinner tables, driving down a country road, and beside the beds of our children.

We find Paul engaging in the ministry of strong proclamation in Acts 17:2-3. "And Paul went in, as was his custom, and on three Sabbath days he reasoned with them from the Scriptures, explaining and proving that it was necessary for the Christ to suffer and to rise from the dead, and saying, 'This Jesus, whom I *proclaim* to you, is the Christ.'" J.I. Packer refers to the gospel as "a proclamation of Divine sovereignty in mercy and judgment, a summons to bow down and worship the mighty Lord on whom man depends for all good ... Its center of reference was unambiguously God."[119] Anything less is a cheap substitute.

Several features of this important ministry are worth noting. First, *strong proclamation must be Christ-centered.* The "him" that we proclaim is Christ—"the hope of glory" (Col. 1:27). This kind of preaching does not water-down the hard edges of the gospel. This kind of preaching does not proclaim a health and wealth "gospel." It does not elevate the free will of the creature. It does not minimize the sovereignty of God. This kind of preaching exalts the living God!

Biblical preaching must be gospel-centered and exalt the glory of God. Biblical preaching proclaims that Jesus died for sinners and was raised for our justification (Rom. 4:25). Biblical preaching proclaims that sinners may be forgiven (Acts 14:48)

---

[119] Introductory essay by J.I. Packer in John Owen, *The Death of Death in the Death of Christ* (Carlisle: The Banner of Truth Trust, reprint 1684), 2.

and proclaims the way of salvation (Acts 16:17). Packer adds, "The preacher's task ... is to display Christ: to explain man's need of him, his sufficiency to save, and his offer of himself in the promises as Savior to all who truly turn to him; and to show as fully and plainly as he can how these truths apply to the congregation before him."[120] Strong biblical proclamation sets Christ in all his glory before every person and pleads with them to find their satisfaction in him!

Second, *strong proclamation must be unabashedly bold.* The apostle Paul models this boldness as he presents the truth of the gospel to the philosophers on Mars Hill:

> *So Paul, standing in the midst of the Areopagus, said: 'Men of Athens, I perceive that in every way you are very religious. For as I passed along and observed the objects of your worship, I found also an altar with this inscription: 'To the unknown god.' What therefore you worship as unknown, this I proclaim to you. The God who made the world and everything in it, being Lord of heaven and earth, does not live in temples made by man, nor is he served by human hands, as though he needed anything, since he himself gives to all mankind life and breath and everything. And he made from one man every nation of mankind to live on all the face of the earth, having determined allotted periods and the boundaries of their dwelling place, that they should seek God, and perhaps feel their way toward him and find him. Yet he is actually not far from each one of us, for 'In him we live and move and have our being ...' (Acts 17:22–28).*

The church needs bold emissaries, men of God who say what they mean and mean what they say. We need men like Polycarp, Tyndale, and Cranmer—men who are willing to lose life and limb for the sake of the gospel. We need men who will stand behind the pulpit and utter the unadulterated gospel of Jesus Christ—men who call sin by name and call sinners to repent. We need men with backbones who herald a timeless message to people in a godless culture.

---

[120] Ibid, 16.

Third, *strong proclamation must be fearless.* We have witnessed the rise of a cowardly culture. These are the days when compromised preachers back-peddle and compromise the precious doctrinal realities of Scripture. We can scarcely remember the days of the Puritans when the doctrines of hell, unconditional election, the sovereignty of God, the ministry of the Holy Spirit, and the lordship of Jesus Christ were powerfully proclaimed from their pulpits. Spurgeon argues:

> *We must preach as men to men, not as divines before clergy and nobility. Preach straight at them. It is of no use to fire your rifle into the sky when your object is to pierce men's hearts. To flourish your sabre finely is a thing which has been done so often that you need not repeat it. Your work is to charge home at the heart and conscience. Fire into the very center of the foe. Aim at effect. 'Oh! oh!' say you, 'I thought we ought never do that.' No, not in the perverted acceptation of the term; but, in the right sense, aim at effect, effect upon the conscience and upon the heart.*[121]

Instead of cowering before men, we need powerful preachers. Instead of pandering to postmodern pundits, we need men who wield the mighty sword of the gospel. In our comprised times, we need men who boldly proclaim the truth of God's Word. We need men who refuse to shrink from declaring God's Word (Acts 20:20).

Fourth, *strong proclamation must be comprehensive.* Faithful men must preach the whole counsel of Scripture. Paul sets the standard in Acts 20:27. He says, "… For I did not shrink from declaring to you the whole counsel of God. This high and holy standard is reaffirmed by the apostle in his letter to Timothy: "I charge you in the presence of God and of Christ Jesus, who is to judge the living and the dead, and by his appearing and his kingdom: preach the word; be ready in season and out of season; reprove, rebuke, and exhort, with complete patience and teaching" (2 Tim. 4:1–2). We simply do not have the luxury of picking and choosing favorites passages to proclaim. Strong

[121] C.H. Spurgeon, *An All-Round Ministry*, 99-100.

proclamation must, therefore, be comprehensive.

Fifth, *strong proclamation must lay the foundation for the Christian worldview.* I remember when the Seattle Mariners began construction of the new baseball stadium in Seattle. Massive pillars were pounded deep into the ground to provide stability for the next architectural wonder of the Emerald City, a field that would accommodate nearly 47,000 baseball fans. I've often reminisced about the early days of construction and compared the gigantic foundational pillars to the core pillars of the Christian worldview. Without these pillars in place, Christians are left to think in bits and pieces. This renders them weak and ineffective as they flounder in theological "no-man's land."

The Christian worldview at its most basic level informs us that *Christ is the creator of all things.* "For by him all things were created, in heaven and on earth, visible and invisible, whether thrones or dominions or rules or authorities - all things were created through him and for him" (Col. 1:16). Charles Darwin resisted this great truth with every fiber of his being. With a few strokes of a pen, his theory of evolution rocked our world and rendered God obsolete. The net result? Darwin essentially vanquished the invisible hand of providence from the public square. Wherever Darwin's worldview gained a hearing, randomness reigned. Instead of the meticulous providence of the Creator God, chaos was the new way of viewing the world.

Christians understand that whenever God is removed or marginalized in the public square, the results are catastrophic. Darwin's relegation of the Creator God to the ash heap leaves people with no basis for knowledge. Additionally, his theory leaves no basis for morality. And evolution leaves men with no basis for meaning. So faithful Christians oppose Darwin's so-called uniformity of natural causes in a closed system with zeal and commit to proclaiming that Christ is the Creator of all things. But we must go further.

Christians maintain that *Christ is the sustainer of all things.* He not only sustains all things; he is sovereign over the free acts of every creature. Proverbs 16:33 explains, "The lot is cast into the lap, but its every decision is from the LORD." Paul continues in his explanation and exaltation of Christ: "And he is before all things, and in him all things hold together" (Col. 1:17). Hebrews 1:3 also demonstrates the sustaining power of Christ over every speck of dust in the universe: "He is the radiance of the glory of God and the exact imprint of his nature, and he upholds the universe by the word of his power ..." So Christ created all things. And Christ sustains all things. Nothing is outside the scope of his providential control.

Additionally, *Christ is the redeemer of sinful people.* "He has delivered us from the domain of darkness and transferred us to the kingdom of his beloved Son, in whom we have redemption, the forgiveness of sins" (Col. 1:13-14). It is our responsibility as God's ambassadors to call sinners to repentance and plead with them to turn to Christ, the only One who has the power to liberate them from the power and penalty of sin.

Finally, *Christ will make all things new.* The apostle John writes:

> *And I heard a loud voice from the throne saying, 'Behold, the dwelling place of God is with man. He will dwell with them, and they will be his people, and God himself will be with them as their God. He will wipe away every tear from their eyes, and death shall be no more, neither shall there be mourning, nor crying, nor pain anymore, for the former things have passed away.' And he who was seated on the throne said, 'Behold, I am making all things new.' Also he said, 'Write this down, for these words are trustworthy and true' (Rev. 21:3-5).*

These are the essential ingredients of the Christian worldview. This worldview, as we discovered in chapter ten, must be promoted and proclaimed by faithful Christians. This worldview provides the necessary foundation for Christians and plays a critical role in the intellectual activity of God-fearing people.

Sixth, *strong proclamation must carry the full weight of biblical authority*. The apostle Paul charges his protégé, Timothy:

> *I charge you in the presence of God and of Christ Jesus, who is to judge the living and the dead, and by his appearing and his kingdom: preach the word; be ready in season and out of season; reprove, rebuke, and exhort, with complete patience and teaching. For the time is coming when people will not endure sound teaching, but having itching ears they will accumulate for themselves teachers to suit their own passions, and will turn away from listening to the truth and wander off into myths (2 Tim. 4:1–4).*

Strong proclamation must convict sinful people. It must admonish them for the sinful acts they commit. Strong proclamation must challenge people to pursue a godly life. It must provide solid instruction that imparts skills that enable people to run hard after God and serve other people. And strong proclamation must confront worldly ideology that opposes God and the principles in Scripture. Lloyd-Jones summarizes the need for strong proclamation. He calls it "logic on fire."[122] May God raise up a new generation of courageous Christians who boldly proclaim the truth that carries the full weight of biblical authority.

Seventh, *strong proclamation must have a sense of urgency.* This proclamation must be blood-earnest and be laced with the weightiness of gravitas. Is this not what is missing from many American pulpits? Open your web browser and scroll through a list of popular preachers. What you are likely to find are a group of men committed to sitting on a bar stool and chatting with their congregations. Instead of hearing the unadulterated, uncompromised Word of God, you will hear about the latest headline, movie, or business book.

It is time for men of God to stand and deliver. It is time to throw away the slippers and bar stools and stand behind a pulpit with an open Bible. It is time to dump the theatrics and declare the Word of God with boldness and confidence. The church has

---

[122] Martin Lloyd-Jones, *Preaching and Preachers* (Grand Rapids: Zondervan Publishing Company, 1971), 97.

no need for levity. The last thing the church needs is cute stories or anecdotes. The church is sick of gutless, faithless, and lazy preachers who care more about the world than the Word of God or the gospel of Jesus Christ.

The holy gravitas of Paul is hard to miss in his address to the Ephesian elders. "Therefore be alert, remembering that for three years I did not cease night or day to admonish every one with tears. And now I commend you to God and to the word of his grace, which is able to build you up and to give you the inheritance among all those who are sanctified" (Acts 20:31-33).

Notice several things about Paul's sense of urgency. *First, he instructs the elders to be alert.* The Greek word means "to beware" or "be watchful." There is a holy earnestness in his attitude as he warns his friends.

Second, Paul is *persistent in his proclamation of the truth.* When he says, "I did not cease night or day to admonish every one with tears" he establishes a pattern that believers in our generation should emulate. That is, we are called to proclaim the truth with faithfulness and persistence.

Third, Paul *passionately proclaims that truth.* He "admonished everyone with tears." *Admonished* comes from the Greek term, *noutheteō, a* word that means "to teach, instruct, or warn." This warning is accompanied by tears, indicating Paul's commitment to passionately proclaim the truth of God's Word. Strong proclamation is not a lecture or a dry recitation of a commentary. Rather, strong proclamation involves a persistent and passionate declaration of the unadulterated truth. Strong proclamation must have a sense of urgency.

Additionally, *strong proclamation must be intensely theological.* Al Mohler addresses pastors in particular: "As a theologian, the pastor must be known for what he teaches as well as what he knows, affirms, and believes. The health of the church depends upon pastors who infuse their congregations with deep biblical and theological conviction, and the primary means of this transfer of conviction is the preaching of the Word of God."[123] Men of God must refuse to water down the truth or marginalize what God has clearly revealed in Scripture. Tragically, however, it is not uncommon to hear preachers who are far removed from theological preaching. These preachers are unfaithful and cowardly. These preachers are spineless.

But pastors are not the only ones who are charged to herald the truth with theological precision. Mohler's admonishment has a direct application for every follower of Christ. We must strive to proclaim God's truth in theological categories that accurately reflect who he is and what he expects from his creatures. This proclamation must be intensely theological.

Finally, *strong proclamation must make a lasting difference in the hearts and minds of people.* Strong proclamation does more than merely fill heads with data and line shelves with notes and annotations. Strong proclamation engages people and equips them. Indeed, strong proclamation transforms their lives.

Paul's commitment to strong proclamation obviously made a deep impact on many people. The closing verses of Acts 20 paint a powerful portrait that we dare not miss: "And when he had said these things, he knelt down and prayed with them all. And there was much weeping on the part of all; they embraced Paul and kissed him, being sorrowful most of all because of the word he had spoken, that they would not see his face again. And they accompanied him to the ship" (Acts 20:36–38). When the Word of God is faithfully and powerfully proclaimed, the lives of people will be revolutionized.

Too often, we view the apostle Paul as a left-brained scholar, a man with a brilliant theological mind who poured over his books and labored in his study. These things are certainly true but Paul's commitment to theology radically impacted both his mind *and* his heart. Consequently, his preaching and teaching deeply moved the people that he taught, preached to,

[123] R. Albert Mohler, *He is Not Silent: Preaching in a Postmodern World* (Chicago: Moody Publishers, 2008), 111.

and trained. The scene in Acts 20 should be lodged in the mind of every Christian and should remind us of the importance of proclaiming truth that makes a lasting difference in the lives of people. Martyn LLoyd-Jones adds, "Preaching should make such a difference to a man who is listening that he is never the same again."[124] Oh, that God would raise up a new generation of Christian leaders who heed this timely counsel!

Serious Warning

Proclaiming Christ involves strong proclamation. But it also involves serious warning as indicated in Colossians 1:29. We have already learned the word *noutheteō*, which is translated as "admonish, instruct, exhort, or warn." One commentator notes, "Admonishing in Scripture has the connotation of confronting with the intent of changing one's attitudes and actions."[125] *Warning people*, as one might imagine, is fraught with controversy and proves to be multi-faceted.

We warn people about the lure of sin and the path of wickedness. We do not have any preconceived notions about the so-called "goodness" of human nature. Rather, we understand that every person is a sinner by nature and choice. Every person has been infected with this deadly virus, which if left unchecked, will maim, kill, and destroy (John 10:10). Apart from redeeming grace, which is received by faith in Christ, sinners will be ruined in this life and judged by a holy God in the life to come. So we warn sinners. We warn them about the folly of sin. Proverbs 16:25 reminds us, "There is a way that seems right to a man, but its end is the way to death." They may enjoy the pleasures of sin for a season but in due course, they will be found out (Numb. 32:23).

James 1:14-15 provides a sobering warning that agrees with

[124] Martyn Lloyd-Jones, *Preaching and Preachers*, 53.

[125] Melick, RR., Philippians, Colossians, Philemon (electronic ed.), *Logos Library System; The New American Commentary* (Nashville: Broadman & Holman Publishers, 2001). The term speaks to the task of calling to mind a correct course of action. It encourages people to get on what they know they need to do.

Solomon and reveals the ultimate destination of a sinful way of life: "But each person is tempted when he is lured and enticed by his own desire. Then desire when it has conceived gives birth to sin, and sin when it is fully grown brings forth death." Thankfully, the elect of God will never reach such a point since we are guarded by the power of God (1 Pet. 1:5) and preserved by the sovereign hand of Jesus (John 10:28).

Nevertheless, we warn people about sin and its temporal and eternal consequences. It is true that the Holy Spirit has a special ministry of conviction. Mark Jones rightly says, "Awareness of sin, conviction of sin, and repentance are glued together by the work of the Holy Spirit, who in God's purposes, leads sinners to Christ by making them aware that they need a Savior."[126] Yet, God has ordained that people come along side in partnership with the Holy Spirit and warn recalcitrant sinners.

Proverbs 4:14-15 says, "Do not enter the past of the wicked, and do not walk in the way of evil. Avoid it; do not go on it, turn away from it and pass on." Steve Lawson concurs: "Sin makes people stupid," he says. Such is the path which is paved by the sinful intentions of men. Our task: Issue a serious warning about the lure of sin and the path of wickedness.

Next, *we warn people to flee from idolatry.* The warning in Hebrews 12:14 is clear: "Strive for peace with everyone, and for the holiness without which no one will see the Lord." Paul instructs the Corinthians to "flee from idolatry" (1 Cor. 6:18). And John warns his readers, "Little children, keep yourselves from idols" (1 John 5:21).

We warn people to steer clear from an evil heart of unbelief. It has been said that "pride is the mother of all sins." However, if we probe deeper, we learn that underneath the grievous sin of pride is the sin of unbelief. Paul identifies the root condition of unbelief by describing hearts that are "hard and impenitent" (Rom. 2:5). The writer of Hebrews urges his readers, "Take care,

---

[126] Mark Jones, *Living for God: A Short Introduction to the Christian Faith* (Wheaton: Crossway Books, 2020), 123-124.

brothers, lest there be in any of you an evil, unbelieving heart, leading you to fall away from the living God" (Heb. 3:12).

Finally, *we warn everyone*. No person is beyond confrontation. We are all sinners. We all need admonition. "If there is sin in the life of a believer," writes John MacArthur, "other believers have the responsibility to lovingly, gently admonish them to forsake that sin."[127]

Systematic Teaching

Proclaiming Christ not only involves strong proclamation and serious warning. It involves systematic teaching. We see the close connection between proclamation and teaching in at the end of the book of Acts: "... *proclaiming* the kingdom of God and *teaching* about the Lord Jesus Christ with all boldness and without hindrance (Acts 28:31).

We are charged to teach continually.[128] Much of this teaching comes through formal instruction in classes, discipleship, catechism, and of course in sermons. Scripture says, "Let the word of Christ dwell in you richly, teaching and admonishing one another in all wisdom, singing psalms and hymns and spiritual songs, with thankfulness in your hearts to God" (Col. 3:16). This kind of systematic teaching finds its origin in the Old Testament:

> *Hear, O Israel: The LORD our God, the LORD is one. You shall love the LORD your God with all your heart and with all your soul and with all your might. And these words that I command you today shall be on your heart. You shall teach them diligently to your children, and shall talk of them when you sit in your house, and when you walk by the way, and when you lie down, and when you rise. You shall bind them as a sign on your hand, and they shall be as frontlets between your eyes. You shall write them on the doorposts of your house and on your gates (Deut. 6:4–9).*

Consequently, we are called to teach everyone with all wis-

---

[127] John F. MacArthur, *Colossians and Philemon*, 79.

[128] This is apparent in the present tense verb, *didáskontes*.

dom—which is to suggest that a good teaching ministry helps people develop godly character and sound judgment over time.

Tragically, parents and even pastors are downplaying or eliminating theological training and education altogether. The abdication of theological education is not only a mistake; it is a serious sin that will have devastating consequences for generations to come. When a human being is not properly fed, the result is physical malnutrition. When a Christian is not properly fed with a proper diet of systematic teaching and preaching, the result is spiritual malnutrition.

PRESENT EVERYONE MATURE IN CHRIST

Paul's first immoveable pillar in Colossians 1:28 is *proclaiming Christ.* The second pillar in verse 28 is to *present everyone mature in Christ.*

Paul's Goal

Paul's aim is to make a presentation. The Greek term translated as *present* (*parísteimi*) is an aorist tense verb and implies that the presentation will occur on the final eschatological day. Imagine a college student who is *presented* before her family and friends at spring commencement. After laboring over her studies, she is *presented* publicly and is conferred with a degree. This is the sense that Paul has in mind, namely, that there will be a *presentation* of the people of God on the last day. And notice that everyone is included. That is, each one of God's elect will be formally presented.

But notice the purpose of this *presentation.* Paul's goal is to present everyone *mature* in Christ. *Téleios* means "perfect, complete, or full grown." The word implies that the goal has been achieved in the way that God planned it. It is a term that ultimately points to spiritual maturity.[129] Paul's goal appears in his letter to the Christians in Ephesus. In the context of chapter 4,

---

[129] The term *téleios is also translated as "perfect" as seen in Matt. 5:48; Rom. 12:2; Jas. 1:4.*

he shows how God raises up pastors and teachers to "equip the saints for the work of the ministry" with the following aim in mind, that they would "attain to the unity of the faith and of the knowledge of the Son of God, to *mature* manhood, to the measure of the stature of the fulness of Christ (Eph. 4:13).

Additionally, Paul refers to the goal of maturity in his letters to the saints in Colossae: "Epaphras, who is one of you, a servant of Christ Jesus, greets you, always struggling on your behalf in his prayers, that you may stand *mature* and fully assured in all the will of God" (Col. 4:12).

To put it mildly, this is a magnanimous moment. This is a presentation of epic proportions! Paul writes triumphantly:

> *And we know that for those who love God all things work together for good, for those who are called according to his purpose. For those whom he foreknew he also predestined to be conformed to the image of his Son, in order that he might be the firstborn among many brothers. And those whom he predestined he also called, and those whom he called he also justified, and those whom he justified he also glorified (Rom. 8:28–30).*

So the good work that God started in his people *will* be completed (Phil. 1:6). Presenting everyone mature in Christ is a settled matter; one that is undergirded by the sovereign plan of God.

Marks of Maturity

Each of us is in process. Every one of God's elect is moving toward the goal of maturity in Christ. We have learned that this goal is guaranteed and will be revealed on the final eschatological day. What are the defining marks of spiritual growth as we move toward the day when we shall be presented as *mature in Christ?*

First, *we must have a God-centered view of God.* The Bible presents a God who exercises sovereign control in creation, providence, and miracles. Proverbs 21:1 illustrates the control of God in vivid terms: "The king's heart is a stream of water in the hand of the LORD; he turns it wherever he will." In Ezra 6:22, the LORD "turned the heart of the king of Assyria." In Ecclesiastes 7:13-14, God' providential control over all things is clearly illustrated: "Consider the work of God: who can make straight what he has made crooked? In the day of prosperity be joyful, and in the day of adversity consider: God has made the one as well as the other, so that man may not find out anything that will be after him." And Ephesians 1:11 reveals the overarching purposes of God in the cosmos: "In him we have obtained an inheritance, having been predestined according to the purpose of him who works all things according to the counsel of his will." Indeed, God exercises sovereign control over all things and all people.

The Westminster Confession of Faith asserts, "God, the Great Creator of all things, doth uphold, direct, dispose, and govern all creatures, actions, and things, from the greatest even to the least, by his most wise and holy providence, according to his infallible foreknowledge, and the free and immutable counsel of his own will, to the praise of the glory of his wisdom, power, justice, goodness, and mercy."[130] In other words, God is the sovereign king who does as he pleases (Ps. 115:3). God reigns (Ps. 99:1-5). His control knows no boundaries. God acts in order to advance his glory (Exod. 14:4). And we rest in the infinite wisdom of God's plan, knowing that his purposes can never be thwarted (Isa. 46:9-10; Job 42:2).

Writers like WM. Paul Young who penned the popular book, *The Shack,* tragically militate against a God who is sovereign over all. Instead of rejoicing in God's sovereignty, Young questions the extent of God's control. He asks a series of questions in his book, *Lies We Believe About God*: "Does God have a wonderful plan for our lives? Does God sit and draw up a perfect will for you and me on some cosmic drafting table, a perfect plan that requires a perfect response? If God then left to react to our stupidity or deafness or blindness or inability, as we constantly

---

[130] G.I. Williamson, *The Westminster Confession of Faith,* 60.

violate perfection through our own presumption?[131] John, one of the characters in Young's novel, *Eve* concurs: "When it comes to plans and purposes, God is not a Draftsman but an Artist, and God will not be apart from us."[132]

Instead of accepting a sovereign God who ordains everything that comes to pass, Young posits a God who reigns by love and relationship alone. Young adds, "The sovereignty of God is not about deterministic control ... Love and relationship trump control every time. Forced love is no love at all."[133]

Charles Hodge disagrees sharply with such a view. The Princeton theologian writes:

> *This is the end which our Lord proposed to himself. He did everything for the glory of God; and for this end, all his followers are required to live and act ... If we make the good of the creature the ultimate object of all God's works, then we subordinate God to the creature, and endless confusion and unavoidable error are the consequence. It is characteristic of the Bible that it places God first, and the good of the creation second.[134]*

A.W. Tozer adds additional clarity and argues, "What comes into our minds when we think about God is the most important thing about us ... So necessary to the church is a lofty concept of God that when that concept in any measure declines, the church with her worship and her moral standards declines along with it. The first step down for any church is taken when it surrenders its high opinion of God."[135] Followers of Christ who desire to move toward maturity, then, must have a God-centered view of God.

Second, *we must have a God-centered view of the gospel.* In

---

[131] WM. Paul Young, *Lies We Believe About God* (New York: Atria Books, 2017), 39.

[132] WM. Paul Young, *Eve* (New York: Howard Books, 2015), 181.

[133] Young, *Lies We Believe About God*, 41.

[134] Charles Hodge, *Systematic Theology – Volume I* (Grand Rapids: Eerdmans Publishing Company, reprint 1995), 536.

[135] A.W. Tozer, *The Knowledge of the Holy* (Lincoln: Back to the Bible, 1961), 1, 4.

recent years, much ink has been spilt by authors who focus on this need. The "gospel-centered" mantra can easily slip into a mere slogan if we aren't careful. This is why Spurgeon's faithful adherence to the gospel and his passion to proclaim it faithfully is so encouraging. The Prince of preachers says:

> *I do not believe we can preach the gospel ... unless we preach the sovereignty of God in His dispensation of grace; nor unless we exalt the electing, unchangeable, eternal, immutable, conquering love of Jehovah; nor do I think we can preach the gospel unless we base it upon the special and particular redemption of His elect and chosen people which Christ wrought out upon the Cross; nor can I comprehend a gospel which lets saints fall away after they are called.[136]*

Notice how Spurgeon moves to the heart of the issue. Desperate times call for desperate measures. The gospel is for sinners who have offended a holy God. Sinners have committed cosmic treason; they have violated God's law. Therefore, the sword of God's judgment will fall swiftly and at any moment. Spurgeon's plea along with all the saints is that sinners would fly to the cross of Christ. Jesus died for sinners so that they might have peace with God and be forgiven all their sin (Acts 4:12; 16:31).

Gospel-centered followers of Christ not only proclaim this message; they live this message until they stand before their Savior! They hold high the name of the Lord Jesus Christ and refuse to compromise the truth. R.C. Sproul writes, "God does not lower his standards to accommodate us."[137] We do well to follow his example as we uphold the gospel, which is God-centered.

Third, *we must have a God-centered view of the church.* It doesn't take much effort to witness the slow and steady erosion of biblical ecclesiology. Frankly, the church is succumbing to the spirit of the age. We have fallen prey to what Francis Schaeffer

---

[136] Charles Haddon Spurgeon, *Autobiography*, Vol. 1, 172.

[137] R.C. Sproul, *The Holiness of God* (Wheaton: Tyndale House Publishers, 1995), 88.

referred to as the "Great Evangelical Disaster."

Calvin remarked that a true church rightly proclaims the Word of God, faithfully administers the sacraments, and disciplines her members. May God help any body of believers who compromises in these critical areas.

SUMMARY

The aim of the apostle Paul was to proclaim Christ in order to present everyone mature in Christ. But all this takes courage and conviction as he sets out to see the people of God grow in maturity. It doesn't happen by accident. It doesn't occur via osmosis. It takes place as Paul moves out in bold obedience and instills a sense of courage and conviction into the hearts of God's people. He militates against spinelessness that surrounds him and so should we.

May Paul's aim be our aim as well. May we develop courage and theological muscle. May our convictions be grounded deeply in the soil of God's Word. And may we grow daily to be the mature men and women that God is calling us to be. Then and only then will we stand apart from those who are spineless.

≫ 14 ≪

STANDING TOGETHER FOR THE GLORY OF CHRIST

—————— ... ——————

*"A life of courageous obedience, no matter what,
is always rooted in a heart that trusts God."*[138]

Paul David Tripp

The film *Rudy* told the tale of Rudy Ruettiger, a scrawny kid from Joliet, Illinois who scrapped his way into the University of Notre Dame. He eventually made his way onto the football team's practice squad. But because of NCAA restrictions, only a certain number of players could suit up for a game, spoiling Rudy's dreams of sprinting onto the field in North Bend. All that changed when his teammates stood together to support the cause of their teammate.

What is it that brings a group of people together to rally around a cause? It never ceases to amaze me what people can accomplish when they stand together. The Bielski brothers defied the Nazis, built a village in the Belarussian forest, and saved 2,000 Jews. A group of Scottish men banded together under the leadership of William Wallace and resisted the tyranny of the British Empire. William Wilberforce rallied like-minded

—————————

[138] Paul David Tripp, *Suffering* (Wheaton: Crossway, 2018), 125.

people together in 18th-century England, which led to the abolition of slavery.

The book of Philippians is a tremendous example of people who stood together during tumultuous times:

- Those who preach with false motives (1:16-17).
- Paul's imprisonment (1:19).
- Impending persecution (1:20-21).
- Opposition from enemies - giving rise to fear (1:28).
- Suffering (1:29).
- Living in a crooked and twisted generation (2:15).
- Risking life and limb (2:30).
- Growling wolves who propagate vicious theological error (3:2).
- Living among enemies of the cross (3:18-19).

2,000 years later - not much has changed. We are bombarded from every angle in our culture. Toeing the line of compromise is commonplace and tolerance of sin is expected. Homosexuality is viewed as an "alternative lifestyle." Partying is encouraged and purity is rejected. Lying and cheating are everyday occurrences while honesty, integrity, and truth-telling are going the way of the dinosaur. The standards of God's Word are marginalized, scoffed at, or thrown out entirely.

Some days are downright discouraging. As Christians, our knees get weak, our resolve grows cold, and we wonder if we will make it. We live in a culture where standing firm doesn't win any popularity contests. But our call before almighty God is to be bold. God calls us to be decisive. He calls us to be unwavering in a world that is drowning in compromise, capitulation, and carnality.

The apostle Paul encouraged his friends in the Philippian church to run strong in the Christian life. In chapter 3, he encourages "Christian runners" to remember the finish line:

- Remember your status - "Our citizenship is in heaven" (3:20).

- Remember your Savior - "We await a Savior, the Lord Jesus" (3:20).

- Remember your salvation - "He will transform your lowly body to be like his glorious body" (3:21).

- Remember your success - Because he wins, we win (3:21).

In Philippians 4, the rally cry of courage and conviction continues as Paul encourages his brothers and sisters to stand together for the glory of Christ.

A COMMITMENT TO STAND FIRM

First, Paul's love for his friends in Philippi is unavoidable as he admonishes them: "Therefore, my brothers, whom I love and long for, my joy and crown, stand firm thus in the Lord, my beloved." (Phil. 4:1). The imperative translated *stand firm* means "to persevere, persist, or maintain one's ground." Think about the resolve of the brave warriors in Leningrad during World War II. Germany came thundering into the Soviet Union and threatened to overtake the city. Many gave in. A few stood firm.

Our Motives for Standing Firm

There are some important reasons for standing firm. The first motive is that Scripture demands it. Three important passages highlight the importance of this biblical command:

> So then, brothers, stand firm and hold to the traditions that you were taught by us, either by our spoken word or by our letter (2 Thess. 2:15).

> By Silvanus, a faithful brother as I regard him, I have written briefly to you, exhorting and declaring that this is the true grace of God. Stand firm in it (1 Pet. 5:12).

> Only let your manner of life be worthy of the gospel of Christ, so that whether I come and see you or am absent, I

*may hear of you that you are standing firm in one spirit,
with one mind striving side by side for the faith of the
gospel ... (Phil.1:27).*

The second motive for standing firm is cultural. Like the believers in Philippi, we live in a depraved generation and face consistent opposition. For example, Christians are routinely persecuted around the world. *Voice of the Martyrs* recently reported the story of a Christ-follower who was fired after he refused to convert to Islam. The most recent report suggests that he is hiding after receiving death threats.[139] The command to stand firm, therefore, is vital for Christians who seek to jettison the spineless path.

Our Model for Standing Firm

The apostle Paul provides several keys for standing firm. First, we must *stand together in harmony* (Phil. 4:2-3). A dispute arose between Euodia and Syntyche - women who labored with Paul in his ministry. He admonishes them to "agree in the Lord" (ESV). He calls them to be like-minded and harmonious. Likewise, the apostle wrote the believers in Corinth: "I appeal to you, brothers, by the name of our Lord Jesus Christ, that all of you agree, and that there be no divisions among you, but that you be united in the same mind and the same judgment" (1 Cor. 1:10). If we intend to stand firm in Christ, we must stand together in harmony.

Second, we must *stand together in joy.* Paul writes, "Rejoice in the Lord always; again I will say, rejoice." (Phil. 4:4). "Joy," writes John MacArthur, "is not a feeling; it is the deep-down confidence that God is in control of everything for the believers good and His own glory, and thus all is well no matter what the circumstances."[140] We must fight for joy together. Matthew Henry adds, "All our joy must terminate in God."

Third, we must *stand together in graciousness.* Paul continues, "Let your reasonableness be known to everyone. The Lord is

[139] https://www.persecution.com/martyr-resources/?_thank_you=Y

[140] John F. MacArthur, *Philippians* (Chicago: Moody Press, 20010, 273.

at hand" (Phil. 4:5). *Reasonableness* comes from a Greek term that is translated as "fair, mild, or gracious." It describes a person with a big heart. Stable and robust faith demands that we are gracious, big-hearted people.

Finally, we must *stand together in the faith*. Paul instructs the Philippians, "Do not be anxious about anything ..." (Phil. 4:6a). *Anxious* means "to be troubled with care." It comes from a word that means "to be divided." C.S. Lewis addresses the problem of anxiety with raw honesty. It "gnaws like fire and loneliness that spreads out like a desert, and the heartbreaking routine of monotonous misery, or again of dull aches that blacken our whole landscape or sudden nauseating pains that knock a man's heart out at one blow ... If I knew a way of escape I would crawl through the sewers to find it."[141]

Anxiety is a constant struggle for many people. People wrestle with anxiety over the basic necessities of life like obtaining the necessary food and clothing. Some people have acute anxiety about their spiritual condition:

> *For when I kept silent, my bones wasted away through my groaning all day long. For day and night your hand was heavy upon me; my strength was dried up as by the heat of summer. I acknowledged my sin to you, and I did not cover my iniquity; I said, 'I will confess my transgressions to the LORD,' and you forgave the iniquity of my sin (Ps. 32:3-5).*

David battled anxiety, which was a product of his sin (Ps. 38:18). Many people struggle with anxious thoughts about the past, the future, or both. But we must refuse to be dominated by anxiety (Matt. 6:27-28, 31, 34; 10:19; Luke 12:22, 25). We must cast all our anxieties on the Savior (1 Pet. 5:7). Indeed, we must stand together in the faith.

Finally, we must *stand together in prayer*. Paul continues in Philippians 4:6, " ... but in everything by prayer and supplication with thanksgiving let your requests be made known to

---

[141] C.S. Lewis, *The Problem of Pain* (San Francisco: HarperCollins Publishers, 1940), 83.

God." Rather than being anxious, then, we are called to present our burdens to God. We are to present every need to God in prayer with thanksgiving. This is to be the habit of our lives.

John Bunyan writes, "Prayer is a sincere, sensible, affectionate pouring out of the heart or soul to God, through Christ, in the strength and assistance of the Holy Spirit, for such things as God has promised, or according to his Word, for the good of the church, with submission in faith to the will of God."[142] When tragedy strikes, we pray. When faced with persecution, we pray. When grief overwhelms us, we pray. When fear invades our souls, we pray. When the stranglehold of anxiety threatens our lives, we pray.

A follower of Christ, then, is committed to standing firm. If we fail to stand together in harmony, there will be division in the church and our evangelistic efforts in the community will be blunted. If we fail to stand together in joy, our lives will be dark and gloomy. If we fail to stand together in graciousness, we will be mean-spirited and play the role of Pharisees. If we fail to stand together in the faith, our resolve will be weak and our trust in God will be small. If we fail to stand together in prayer, our lives will be powerless. And if we fail to stand firm in the Lord, the gospel will lose its flavor! The irony is that the only way we can make a commitment to stand firm is by clinging to Christ and appropriating the promises of the gospel.

A CHARACTER CONTROLLED BY CHRIST

A follower of Christ not only makes a commitment to stand firm; he or she has a character controlled by Christ. Philippians 4:7 reveals the results of such commitment: "And the peace of God, which surpasses all understanding, will guard your hearts and your minds in Christ Jesus." The result is a peaceful disposition.

A Peaceful Disposition

The *peace of God* is "a state of tranquility, security, and safety." Here we are assured of our salvation through Christ alone. Jesus

142 John Bunyan, *Prayer* (Edinburgh: The Banner of Truth Trust, 1662), 13.

reassured his disciples, "Peace I leave with you; my peace I give to you. Not as the world gives do I give to you. Let not your hearts be troubled, neither let them be afraid" (John 14:27). Later in John 16:33, Jesus said, "I have said these things to you, that in me you may have peace. In the world you will have tribulation. But take heart; I have overcome the world." And Isaiah reminds us of the great hope we have as we trust in God's provision. "You keep him in perfect peace whose mind is stayed on you, because he trusts in you" (Isa. 26:3).

This is an *earth-shattering peace* that surpasses all understanding. It is a peace that can never be obtained through philosophy, substances, relationships, possessions, or even religion! This is the peace of God that we receive through Christ!

This is a *peace that protects*. Paul reveals that this peace guards our hearts and minds in Christ Jesus. God's peace guards our hearts and minds from anxiety. We are delivered from worrying about the next recession, joblessness, wayward children, illness, strained relationships, and persecution.

Rudy's teammates stood together for their friend in his time of need. Oh, Christian—I urge you to stand together for the glory of Christ for the great cause of the gospel. Are you a follower of Christ? If you have not yet made peace with God, your life will not be characterized by peace. The Bible says that "the way of peace they have not yet known" (Rom. 3:17). "To set the mind on the flesh is death, but to set the mind on the Spirit is life and peace" (Rom. 8:6). Christ died so that you might know God, be reconciled to God, and be forgiven of all your sin. He died and was raised to life on the third day so that you might have peace with God (Rom. 5:1).

Followers of Christ are committed to standing firm and possess a character that is controlled by Christ. Such a person is able, by God's grace, to steer clear from spineless living.

NEVER SURRENDER

...

"Only let your manner of life be worthy of the gospel of Christ, so that whether I come and see you or am absent, I may hear of you that you are standing firm in one spirit, with one mind striving side by side for the faith of the gospel..."

Philippians 1:27

I n the dark hours of World War II, Winston Churchill led his countrymen with steely strength and valor. In the midst of a crippling enemy invasion, the Prime Minister stood before the British Parliament and delivered a riveting speech that galvanized a nation:

Even though large tracts of Europe and many old and famous States have fallen or may fall into the grip of the Gestapo and all the odious apparatus of Nazi rule, we shall not flag or fail. We shall go on to the end. We shall fight in France, we shall fight on the seas and oceans, we shall fight with growing confidence and growing strength in the air, we shall defend our island, whatever the cost may be. We shall fight on the beaches, we shall fight on the landing grounds, we shall fight in the fields and in the streets, we shall fight in the hills; we shall never surrender, and even if, which I do not for a moment believe, this island or a large part of it were subjugated and starving, then our

Empire beyond the seas, armed and guarded by the British Fleet, would carry on the struggle, until, in God's good time, the new world, with all its power and might, steps forth to the rescue and the liberation of the old.[143]

Churchill didn't flinch. He didn't compromise. He didn't equivocate or hedge his bets. Instead, he set his eyes on the goal of victory as he led his nation with bold resolve and courage. Surrender was not an option for Winston Churchill.

In a similar way, Paul the apostle emboldened and encouraged the church in Philippi. These believers were likely struggling with fear and were growing weary in the face of adversity. Some of these believers, no doubt, were tempted to give up the Christian race entirely.

Paul addresses his brothers and sisters in Philippi from the confines of a Roman jailhouse and seeks to galvanize their perspective and renew their hope. He reminds them of their partnership in the gospel (Phil. 1:3-5). He reminds them that God will complete the good work that he started in them (Phil. 1:6). He assures them that his prayers are focused like a laser beam on them, which are concerned for their spiritual well-being (Phil.1:9-11). Paul assures his friends that his incarceration has a gospel-centered motive. In fact, he reminds them that his chains are actually emboldening followers of Christ to "speak the word without fear" and that the progress of the gospel will not be hindered (Phil. 1:12-18). And he offers them fresh perspective regarding the gospel:

> *...for I know that through your prayers and the help of the Spirit of Jesus Christ this will turn out for my deliverance, as it is my eager expectation and hope that I will not be at all ashamed, but that with full courage now as always Christ will be honored in my body, whether by life or by death. For to me to live is Christ, and to die is gain. If I am to live in the flesh, that means fruitful labor for me. Yet which I shall choose I cannot tell. I am hard*

[143] Winston Churchill, cited in Anthony McCarten, *Darkest Hour: How Churchill Brought England Back From the Brink* (New York: Harper, 2017), 254-255.

pressed between the two. My desire is to depart and be with Christ, for that is far better. But to remain in the flesh is more necessary on your account. Convinced of this, I know that I will remain and continue with you all, for your progress and joy in the faith, so that in me you may have ample cause to glory in Christ Jesus, because of my coming to you again (Phil. 1:19–26).

In the verses that follow, Paul focuses on the power of the gospel. For it is the gospel that will mobilize the feet of the Philippians. It is the gospel that will empower their ministry. It is the gospel that will fuel their resolve:

Only let your manner of life be worthy of the gospel of Christ, so that whether I come and see you or am absent, I may hear of you that you are standing firm in one spirit, with one mind striving side by side for the faith of the gospel, and not frightened in anything by your opponents. This is a clear sign to them of their destruction, but of your salvation, and that from God. For it has been granted to you that for the sake of Christ you should not only believe in him but also suffer for his sake, engaged in the same conflict that you saw I had and now hear that I still have (Phil. 1:27–30).

The believers in Philippi were undergoing a season of persecution. Their faith was being tested. Have you been there? Are you there now? Have you experienced the pain of discouragement and felt the sting of defeat? Have you struggled in the Christian life and wondered if you would ever rise above it all and showcase the glory of God? When your opponents marginalize you, do you feel like a spiritual weakling? Is your courage waning? Are your convictions fading?

These are the kinds of questions that plagued the Philippians. Clearly, they were deeply encouraged to read Paul's epistle. In this section of Paul's letter, he sets forth the marks of a spiritual powerhouse. These marks, all of which are undergirded by the gospel, will strengthen the spiritual muscles of the Philippians believers. Like Churchill, they will never surrender!

EXEMPLARY CONDUCT

The apostle begins by establishing an imperative: "Only let your *manner of life* be worthy of the gospel of Christ, so that whether I come and see you or am absent, I may hear of you that you are standing firm in one spirit, with one mind striving side by side for the faith of the gospel …" (Phil. 1:27). Such conduct is characterized by faithful striding, faithful standing, and faithful striving.

Faithful Striding

The apostle begins his high-octane encouragement by urging the Philippians to live lives that are "worthy of the gospel of Christ." The Greek phrase translated as *manner of life* means "to be a citizen or to pledge to live accordingly." It is a political term that spoke deeply to the Philippians who lived in the midst of Roman culture. But the term means more than mere citizenship. Paul's mandate is that they live in a manner that is worthy of the gospel of Jesus Christ. Likewise, he charges the Ephesians to walk in a *worthy* manner (Eph. 4:1). And he admonishes the Thessalonian believers to do the same: "For you know how, like a father with his children, we exhorted each one of you and encouraged you and charged you to walk in a manner *worthy* of God, who calls you into his own kingdom and glory" (1 Thess. 2:11-12).

This faithful striding involves walking in newness of life. "We were buried therefore with him by baptism into death, in order that, just as Christ was raised from the dead by the glory of the Father, we too might walk in newness of life" (Rom. 6:4). Faithful striding involves walking in purity. "Let us walk properly as in the daytime, not in orgies and drunkenness, not in sexual immorality and sensuality, not in quarreling and jealousy" (Rom. 13:13). Faithful striding involves walking by faith (2 Cor. 5:7). Faithful striding means walking according to the Spirit (Gal. 5:16). It involves walking in love (Eph. 5:2), walking as children of light (Eph. 5:8), and walking carefully (Eph.

5:15). Indeed, this faithful striding that Paul demands involves walking in truth (3 John 1:4).

Faithful Standing

Exemplary conduct involves not only faithful striding; it involves faithful standing. Paul continues in Philippians 1:27. He writes, "I may hear of you that you are *standing firm* in one spirit, with one mind ..." *Standing firm* (*steikete*) means "to persevere; to persist; to maintain your ground." Paul uses the same word in other New Testament passages. "*Stand fast* in the Lord," he writes (1 Thess. 3:8). "*Stand firm,*" he writes to the Galatian church (Gal. 5:1; c.f. Phil. 4:1). "So then, brothers, *stand firm* and hold to the traditions that you were taught by us, either by our spoken word or by our letter" (2 Thess 2:15). "*Stand firm* in the faith; act like men" (1 Cor. 16:13).

In our generation, we commit ourselves to standing firm for the church. That is, we stand firm for biblical truth: "I hope to come to you soon, but I am writing these things to you so that, if I delay, you may know how one ought to behave in the household of God, which is the church of the living God, a pillar and buttress of the truth" (1 Tim. 3:14–15). We stand firm for the authority of the Scriptures. Francis Shaeffer raised the evangelical bar at a time when biblical morality was fading and fervor for Scripture was eroding: "Holding to a strong view of Scripture or not holding to it is the watershed of the evangelical world."[144] Therefore, we commit to standing firm to a lifestyle of godliness.

Faithful Striving

Exemplary conduct in the church of Jesus Christ involves faithful striding and faithful standing. But Paul goes one step further. He admonishes the Philippians to "strive side by side." *Strive* comes from the Greek word, *sunathlountes* which means "to fight together for a common purpose." In this case, they are called upon to "strive side by side for the faith of the gospel." The

[144] Francis Schaeffer, *No Final Conflict* (Downers Grove: Intervarsity, 1976), 13.

NIV84 translates this phrase as "contending as one man for the faith of the gospel." That is, faithful striving involves determination and hard work.[145]

There is not a hint of *giving up* or *capitulating* to the culture. Paul is bound and determined to spur his fellow believers on and motivate them to striving together, all for the sake of the gospel. An example of faithful striving is Cliff Barrows, the longtime associate of Billy Graham. In 1947, Mr. Barrows began his ministry in the *Billy Graham Evangelistic Association,* where he would serve over sixty years. Barrows not only helped facilitate worship at Dr. Graham's crusades; he also served as the host of the *Hour of Decision* radio program. Billy Graham spoke in glowing terms about his faithful friend, much like Paul referred to Epaphroditus as a "fellow worker and fellow soldier" (Phil. 2:25) Graham spoke glowingly about his faithful friend, Cliff Barrows: "His uncanny ability to lead a Crusade choir of thousands of voices or an audience of a hundred thousand voices in a great hymn or Gospel chorus is absolutely unparalleled."[146] But Graham was quick to point out that earthly talent was not the secret to Barrows' effectiveness in ministry: "It is his humility and his willingness to be a servant, which spring from his devotional life and his daily walk with Christ. The love of Christ so monopolizes his heart and will that he never seeks his own advantage at the expense of others or puts another person down."[147] Such is the life of a man committed to faithful striving.

So the first mark of a courageous Christian in Philippians 1:27-30 is exemplary conduct which involves faithful striding, faithful standing, and faithful striving. One man who modeled

---

[145] Note that Paul utilizes the same word in Philippians 1:27 and Philippians 4:3 where he writes, "Yes, I ask you also, true companion, help these women, who have labored (*sunathlountes*) side by side with me in the gospel together with Clement and the rest of my fellow workers, whose names are in the book of life" (Phil. 4:3, ESV).

[146] Billy Graham, *Just as I Am: The Autobiography of Billy Graham* (Grand Rapids: Zondervan, 2011), 672.

[147] Ibid, 673.

this kind of approach to the Christian life was Francis Schaeffer. His conduct was exemplary, indeed. He faithfully stood for biblical truth and the battle for the inerrancy of Scripture. He faithfully opposed the theological liberalism and neo-orthodoxy of the 50's and 60's. Speaking at a memorial service in London, Os Guinness said that the greatest thing about Francis Schaeffer was Francis Schaeffer."[148] Guinness identified something in Schaeffer that was difficult to miss. Schaeffer was a courageous Christian.

Are you a courageous Christian? Are you known for your exemplary conduct? Never forget that your exemplary conduct is centered around the gospel of the Lord Jesus Christ. The gospel is nothing less than Jesus's life which was lived to the glory of God, who paid for sinners with his precious blood on the cross. Our Savior was buried and raised from the dead on the third day (1 Cor. 15:3-4) and promises to grant eternal life to everyone who believes. This is what we stride for. This is what we stand for. And this is what we strive for, namely, the gospel of Jesus Christ!

When tempted to engage in behavior that is not worthy of the gospel, I urge you to commit yourself to exemplary conduct. When the crowd pressures you to fit into their worldly mold, I urge you to live to the glory of God. And when you get tired, discouraged and feel like quitting the race, I implore you to live a life of exemplary behavior by faithful striding, standing, and striving along with like-minded brothers and sisters for the great cause of Christ.

EXTRAORDINARY COURAGE

Exemplary conduct is not the only matter that concerns Paul. He also wants to inspire the Philippian believers to be a people of extraordinary courage. He adds, " … and not frightened in anything by your opponents. This is a clear sign to them of their destruction, but of your salvation, and that from God. For it has

---

[148] Os Guinness, Cited in Colin Duriez, *Francis Schaeffer: An Authentic Life* (Wheaton: Crossway Books, 2008), 204.

been granted to you that for the sake of Christ you should not only believe in him but also suffer for his sake, engaged in the same conflict that you saw I had and now hear that I still have" (Phil. 1:28–30).

Recognizing Our Opponents

In the 1st-century, the opponents of Christians would add human works to the gospel. For instance, in Philippians 3:2, Paul warns his friends, "Look out for the dogs, look out for the evildoers, look out for those who mutilate the flesh." Like the false teachers in Galatia, these dangerous teachers were advocating the practice of circumcision for salvation. In one sentence, Paul presents three imperatives: *Look out* comes from the Greek, *blepō*, a term that suggests careful evaluation or warning.

In the twenty-first century, Paul's command to *look out* is no less important. We must be on our guard against every worldview that is antithetical to the Christian faith. But we must especially be on the *lookout* for opponents within the church. We must beware of those whose eyes have been glazed over by pragmatic ministry models that cater to the flesh. We must be beware of those who reject propositional truth or downplay orthodoxy. We must beware of anyone who downplays the importance of expository preaching. We must be on guard against anyone who blurs or obliterates the roles of men and women in the church as well as the home. We must beware of those who promote universal reconciliation, a view that is gaining in popularity. For instance, Gerry Beauchemin writes, "For sooner or later, all will come to faith and obedience."[149] Beuchemin refers to hell as "a horrid doctrine."[150] Obviously, such views are foreign to Scripture. Therefore, these views should be rejected.[151]

---

[149] Gerry Beauchemin, *Hope Beyond Hell* (Olmito: Malista Press, 2007), 94.

[150] Ibid, 17.

[151] See James W. Walraven, *Will God Save Everyone: Christian Universalism, Hell, Heaven and the Scriptures* (Enumclaw: Redemption Press, 2020).

Responding to Our Opponents

It is not enough to merely recognize our opponents. We must also respond to their foolishness and false teaching. Paul's counsel to Christians is encouraging and inspires boldness. First, *we respond with fearlessness. Frightened* in verse 28 comes from the Greek term *pturómenoi* which is translated as "timid or fearful." In other words, Paul encourages his Philippian friends to never be intimidated by their opponents. The CSB translation is helpful: " … not being frightened in any way by your opponents." Therefore, Christians are to take heart even in the face of false teachers. Notice that Paul says the result of our fearless response will be a "clear sign of their destruction" and a sign of our salvation. Instead of cowering in fear, then, when false teachers surround us we should respond courageously and thus receive assurance of our salvation.

Second, *our response involves suffering.* "For it has been granted to you that for the sake of Christ you should not only believe in him but also suffer for his sake …" (Phil. 1:29). To *suffer* (*páschein*), is to experience harm or emotional pain. No one ever promised a life of ease in the Christian life. Faithful and decisive response to false teachers will involve suffering. They will attack us. They will misrepresent us. They will seek to discredit us. They will work with all their might to undermine us. Indeed, anyone who responds courageously to opponents of the Christian faith will endure seasons of suffering.

It is important to understand that this suffering has been *granted* to us. *Granted* is a term that means "to give graciously as a sign of goodwill." We have been bestowed, then, with the gracious gift of faith *and* suffering. Such a gift should fortify our souls with courage, then, knowing that the sovereign God of the universe has ordained these things to come to pass.

This promised suffering also has a specific purpose. Paul says that we "suffer for his sake" (v. 29). That is, we suffer for the sake of the Lord Jesus. Our sufferings are small in comparison to the suffering that Jesus endured on the cross for our sins, but ours is real suffering, nonetheless. There is a price to pay for courage. There is a price to pay for conviction. But suffer we will for the great namesake of the Lord Jesus Christ.

Finally, *we know we are not alone.* Paul makes it clear in verse 30 that we are engaged in the same conflict as he. Even in the midst of suffering, we are assured that Paul too faced opposition from his opponents. Paul's response to suffering should instill us with great confidence as we move forward in our Christian journey.

In his recent book *The Gathering Storm,* Al Mohler raises the bar for followers of Christ. He warns us to steer clear from every form of compromise and encourages us to be strong and courageous:

> *Where you find failing churches and denominations, you find a loss of faith in God. Where you find courage, conviction, and steadfastness, you find the people of God with vibrant faith in Christ and his promises. In this secular age, Christians must display faith in at least three ways: faith in God's design, faith in God's Word, and faith in the power of the gospel.*[152]

A spiritual powerhouse demonstrates exemplary conduct and extraordinary courage. The only way to live with this kind of spiritual power is to walk in daily fellowship with Christ. It is only in Christ that you can demonstrate exemplary conduct and extraordinary courage.

My prayer is that you would strive to be a man or woman of courage and conviction. As you survey the ecclesiastical land-

---

[152] R. Albert Mohler, *The Gathering Storm* (Nashville: Nelson Books, 2020), 191.

scape, you will no doubt see spinelessness on the horizon. You will be encouraged to join in the cowardly parade. But you know better. You are prepared to fight. You are prepared to stand up for righteousness. You are prepared to suffer for Christ's sake. You will never surrender. The path of spinelessness is no longer an option for you!

CONCLUSION

--- ... ---

J. C. Ryle warns, "Take away the gospel from a church and that church is not worth preserving. A well without water, a scabbard without a sword, a steam-engine without a fire, a ship without compass and rudder, a watch without a mainspring, a stuffed carcass without life, all these are useless things. But there is nothing so useless as a church without the gospel."[153]

Ryle's warning to the Church of England in the 19th-century is no less of a challenge in our generation. We have evolved into a spineless culture, accepting error, tolerating sin, and capitulating to the spirit of the age. Our cowardice has paid crippling dividends, which are cascading through the church and lead to further discouragement and decay. Our flimsy convictions teach our children that truth does not matter and that God's Word is negotiable. It is no wonder that millennials are so tethered to mediocrity and glued to mindless trivia and minutia.

These days, which are marked by a tepid and cowardly "Christianity" must end. The days of "spineless Christianity" must draw to a close. Now is the time for a new generation of leaders to stand up and proclaim the truth with courage and conviction. We must broadcast the truth, even when it is unpopular. Now is the time to buckle our helmets and enter the battle-

---

[153] J.C. Ryle, *Light from Old Times* (Edinburgh: The Banner of Truth, 2015), 45.

field with courage and conviction. We must obey the mandate set forth by the apostle Peter:

> *Therefore, preparing your minds for action, and being sober-minded, set your hope fully on the grace that will be brought to you at the revelation of Jesus Christ. As obedient children, do not be conformed to the passions of your former ignorance, but as he who called you is holy, you also be holy in all your conduct, since it is written, 'You shall be holy, for I am holy' (1 Pet. 1:13-16).*

John Bunyan's courageous character, *Evangelist* offered a sober warning and words of encouragement to pilgrims who sought the narrow path of courage and conviction:

> *Therefore, you will soon enter a town that you will in time see before you. In that town you'll be severely besieged by enemies who will try hard in their attempts to kill you, and you can be sure that one or both of you must seal with the blood of the testimony that you hold.*

> *But be faithful even to the point of death, and (the King) will give you the crown of life ... When you arrive at the town and find fulfilled what I've told you here, then remember your friend and 'be men of courage; commit yourselves to your faithful Creator and continue to do good.[154]*

The path of courage and conviction will be filled with pain and persecution. This path will be marked by resistance and scorn. Indeed, all who blaze a trail of biblical faithfulness will be met by fierce opposition. The prophets, apostles, Reformers, Huguenots, and Puritans remind us that anyone who has the audacity to obey God will be met with fierce antagonism. Any Christ-follower who maintains allegiance to God will pay a steep price. Surely, the price of persecution is costly and may even result in martyrdom. Yet, Scripture helps us in our time of need by pointing us to the promise of an eternal reward. At the end of this earthly journey, Paul the apostle contemplates the prospect of crossing the finish line. He joyfully anticipates the breaking of the "heavenly tape" where he will be ushered into eternity:

[154] John Bunyan, The Pilgrim's Progress (Gainesville: Bridge-Logos, 1998), 113.

For I am already being poured out as a drink offering, and the time of my departure has come. I have fought the good fight, I have finished the race, I have kept the faith. Henceforth there is laid up for me the crown of righteousness, which the Lord, the righteous judge, will award to me on that Day, and not only to me but also to all who have loved his appearing (2 Tim. 4:6–8).

Hugh Latimer offers timely encouragement that serves us well in our generation: "Be of good comfort, Master Ridley, and play the man; we shall this day, by God's grace, light such a candle in England as I trust shall never be put out."[155] Isaac Ambrose reminds us, "Not one of all his true soldiers was ever left to perish on the field of battle. Put on courage, ye Christian warriors! Fight the good fight of faith, be faithful unto death, and then, your Captain will release you from the war, and give you the crown of life, which you shall forever wear, in honor of your gracious Lord and Savior.[156] May the same be said of every follower of Christ. The choice before us is a matter of grave importance. Will we tread on the path of the spineless? Or will we stand and be counted? Will we be numbered among the courageous? Will we be known for our biblical convictions? May the sovereign LORD restore courage and conviction to our generation. And may courage and conviction be transferred to our children and grandchildren so that God might be greatly glorified.

Soli Deo Gloria!

---

[155] Hugh Latimer, cited in J.C. Ryle, *Light from Old Times* (Edinburgh: The Banner of Truth Trust, 2015), 27.

[156] Isaac Ambrose, *The Christian Warrior: Wrestling with Sin, Satan, the World and the Flesh* (Digital Puritan Press, 2012), Loc. 34.